RULES *of* *the* GAME

RULES *of* *the* GAME

HOW TO SUCCEED

in Life's Most Important Investment and Endeavor,

MARRIAGE

LAWRENCE & XINIA
OTAROLA

New York

RULES *of* *the* GAME

HOW TO SUCCEED
in Life's Most Important Investment and Endeavor,
MARRIAGE

© 2017 LAWRENCE OTAROLA.

Originally printed in Spanish as "10 Reglas del Juego: Matrimonio, la Empresa de la Vida" © 2009 Lawrence Otarola

Published in New York, New York, by Morgan James Publishing. Morgan James and The Entrepreneurial Publisher are trademarks of Morgan James, LLC.
www.MorganJamesPublishing.com

The Morgan James Speakers Group can bring authors to your live event. For more information or to book an event visit The Morgan James Speakers Group at www.TheMorganJamesSpeakersGroup.com.

Shelfie

A **free** eBook edition is available
with the purchase of this print book.

CLEARLY PRINT YOUR NAME ABOVE IN UPPER CASE

Instructions to claim your free eBook edition:
1. Download the Shelfie app for Android or iOS
2. Write your name in **UPPER CASE** above
3. Use the Shelfie app to submit a photo
4. Download your eBook to any device

ISBN 978-1-63047-908-4 paperback
ISBN 978-1-63047-910-7 eBook
ISBN 978-1-63047-909-1 hardcover
Library of Congress Control Number:
2015920587

Cover Design by:
Rachel Lopez
www.r2cdesign.com

Interior Design by:
Bonnie Bushman
The Whole Caboodle Graphic Design

In an effort to support local communities and raise awareness and funds, Morgan James Publishing donates a percentage of all book sales for the life of each book to Habitat for Humanity Peninsula and Greater Williamsburg.

Get involved today, visit
www.MorganJamesBuilds.com

**Habitat
for Humanity®**
Peninsula and
Greater Williamsburg
Building Partner

Xinia and I would like to dedicate this book to all the couples that God has brought across our path and the way they transparently shared their mistakes and successes, enriching our understanding of the most important investment and endeavor in life.

To all those who pursue success in their marriage partnership and are seeking ways of enriching it, to those who might find in these pages the insight and tools that allow them to see the light at the end of the tunnel.

Finally, I cannot let this opportunity go without deeply and sincerely thanking my marriage partner, the one who has been so patient and forgiving, who has given me the best years of her life and the greatest children in the world, the one who keeps fueling my days, my one and only Xinia, whose name's meaning describes her so well: hospitable.

CONTENTS

Preface   ix

Introduction   xvi

STATE OF THE BUSINESS   1

Be Aware of the Risk Sources   3

Risk Source One: Background   5

Risk Source Two: Marriage of Our Parents   8

Risk Source Three: Past Relationships   13

Risk Source Four: Religion   16

Risk Source Five: Finances   19

Risk Source Six: Age   23

Risk Source Seven: Support Network   26

Risk Source Eight: Period of Change   30

Risk Source Nine: Compatibility   33

RULES OF THE GAME   37

Rule of the Game One: Regard Marriage as a   39
    One-of-a-Kind Contract

Rule of the Game Two: Regard Marriage as an   53
    Ongoing Partnership

Rule of the Game Three: Have Values as the Driving Fuel   63

Rule of the Game Four: Cut the Umbilical Cord 75

Rule of the Game Five: Glue Together As One 83

Rule of the Game Six: Exercise Frontline Leadership 90

Rule of the Game Seven: Exercise Influential Leadership 100

Rule of the Game Eight: Own Your Incapacities 109

Rule of the Game Nine: Become a Threefold Cord 119

Rule of the Game Ten: Leave a Legacy Behind 126

About the Authors 135

Notes 137

PREFACE

Several years ago, while waiting for a friend to arrive at the Raleigh-Durham International Airport, I engaged an elderly woman, seated next to me in the waiting area, in conversation. She talked about her five children, sixteen grandchildren, and seven great-grandchildren. At one point she asked, "What do you do for a living, Lawrence?"

"I write about marriage and conduct seminars on family issues," I replied.

She leaned back and gave me that look—you know what I am talking about. Then she said, "Son, whatever you want to know about family, just ask me."

I have no doubt the lady at the airport knew a thing or two about marriage and family issues, in fact, she was the real expert. My wife, Xinia, and I, are not the experts, the "know-it-all couple" when it comes to marriage. We have yet to figure out many aspects of marriage. We haven't enjoyed the benefit of being highly compatible; nor did we grow up in healthy homes that modeled an extraordinary sense of love and commitment. In fact, all the odds were against us long before we entered an agreement to love and cherish one another "until death do us part."

I come from a rather dysfunctional family, with poor values about marriage, children, and family. The majority of my uncles and aunts are divorced; they've struggled with alcohol, unfaithfulness, and emotional and physical abuse as aggressors or victims of aggression. On the other hand, Xinia comes from a family that never considers divorce an option. However, Xinia watched her mother willingly sacrifice all she had for her children—but not for her husband. Consequently, Xinia learned a lot about being a mother but not so much about being a wife.

Xinia and I have gone through many ups and downs. We have faced interference from family members and friends, disappointment, resentment, illness, incompatibility, strong differences in perceptions and values, financial struggles, and drastic changes throughout the life of our marriage. In spite of all these detrimental factors, we have built a better marriage every year since 1986, when we promised each other that, for better or for worse, we will be together. The secret of our success lies in the strong belief that marriage and family are our most important investments in life. To us, marriage really is a very serious business. We strongly believe that the current cultural understanding of marriage, and the solutions and approaches to its struggles, are the product of a mix of several distorted and destructive perceptions generated by a shift of values and beliefs. We suggest that a back-to-the-basics approach could provide great insights and new ways of seeing and doing marriage.

Our approach regards marriage as a life project, as an endeavor similar to that of two entrepreneurs who want to start their dream life project, as a long-term investment that requires patience, consistency, and a lifelong period to harvest its benefits. We also strongly believe that such an approach gives many husbands the chance to more enthusiastically engage in their marriages because they can relate more to the familiar "language" of business, in contrast to the usual psychological approach prevailing today that it's harder to digest by most men. No wonder many husbands seem to drag their feet to these workshops, seminars, and counseling sessions agreeing to participate solely to make their spouse content.

Speaking about this connection between business and marriage, I learned the following information while on a flight to Santa Cruz, Bolivia back in 2008, on my way to talk about marriage during a TV appearance:

- According to the Small Business Administration Office of Advocacy, 600,000 optimistic entrepreneurs start new businesses every year, even when about 600,000 businesses fail every year.[1]
- According to Brian Tracy, "at least 90 percent of new businesses succeed if their founders are experienced entrepreneurs—the ones who have figured out the rules and make decisions based on those rules."[2]

Looking out the airplane window, flying above a peaceful and endless bed of clouds, I pondered these facts trying to connect them with my thoughts about the TV interview I was going to have, and all of the sudden, it hit me. I realized that many regard marriage as obsolete because one out of every two marriages ends in divorce, but nobody thinks the "free market" model is obsolete, even though the business turnover rate is twice that of marriage. Why is this?

In the business world, most people understand that the problem is not with the "free market" model, but rather with those who don't know the "rules of the game" as they apply in the business world. Likewise, in marriage, if we know the rules of the game and its risks we are more likely to succeed. It's really no more complicated than that. Like any other activity in life, to achieve success we must learn the rules that pertain to the activity, acquire the requisite skills to engage in it, and develop the commitment to apply these appropriately. Our plans and choices must be carefully thought out and executed.

If you attempt to fly an airplane without any training or education, you will likely have difficulty getting it off the ground, much less sustaining the ideal altitude. And yet how often do we try to establish a successful marriage without the appropriate training and knowledge of its best practices? It's often as if we are trying to "wing it." We expect to put our marriage on autopilot and everything will work out fine, relying on our feelings or our preconceptions, which are often based on what we have witnessed in the unsuccessful marriages of others. Then we wonder why our marriage isn't working. Like the pilot in an aircraft, we need to know the rules of the game, the rules that will lead us to a successful marriage.

In today's society, young people are waiting later to get married, believing that the problem is in the model. They hear that nearly 50 percent of marriages end in divorce. What they do not hear, or most likely ignore, is that researchers noticed divorce rates decreasing among the better educated. We might consider the fact that we have been placing the problem on the wrong source. It is not the model or the age but the lack of education and training. People go to school to get an education or a certification or a license. However, we jump into life's most important investment and endeavor without any training or real knowledge of best practices and core principles, what we call the "Rules of the Game."

When our children were young, Xinia and I encouraged them to participate in sports. Our youngest daughter looked hopelessly lost in her early softball tryouts. At first, she had no frame of reference whatsoever for the game. What she initially needed was to learn the rules of the game. In our home country of Costa Rica, we have a saying, "Before you play ball, you must paint the field." This means that before you become involved in any work, family, or economic relationship, you must define the terms and expectations of that relationship. In this book, you will learn the Rules of the Game and the risks involved in such endeavor. You will gain a clearer understanding of what marriage is really all about. You will learn how to "play fair." You will understand what it takes to be successful in this wonderful encounter between two people who love each other and dare to risk everything in order to undertake life's most important enterprise: marriage.

This is the reason why we started a movement to persuade our generation and future generations that marriage is, and will continue to be, very serious business. This is done by getting a hold on the most serious and recent social research, best practices for successful and healthy homes, principles and laws of universal application, and tools and processes used in the business world.

We hope to spark a worldwide movement of marriage partners that teach young people what marriage really is, how to choose a partner for life, and what partnership model is by far the best. We hope that every home becomes a place where other couples are taught what the risk sources are, what the Rules of the Game are, and how to build a solid marriage partnership. In addition, we hope to help those who have experienced the pain, failure, and loss of a separation and how to get up and rebuild a strong and vibrant marriage partnership. We started this movement under the banner of Marriage, Serious Business.

Marriage, Serious Business (www.MarriageSeriousBusiness.com) will shift the typical perception of marriage by relating it to the skills and kind of investment needed by an entrepreneur to start and sustain a thriving, vibrant, profitable business. We believe these concepts can produce a domino effect, triggering a series of escalated changes in families all around the world. This shift in perception towards a business view of marriage will transform how you value your family. These new attitudes will also likely alter how you feel. Though the way you feel may or may not ultimately be critical in the process, how you feel will help transform the way you behave.

The goal of Marriage, Serious Business is to create an enduring sense of marriage entrepreneurship within you so that you willingly modify and transform your behavior in order to take the steps required in a persevering and successful marriage. The reason most couples today are giving up prematurely is because they ignore the great benefits of staying together. According to Linda J. Waite and Maggie Gallagher, in their book *Why Married People Are Happier, Healthier, and Better Off Financially*, "86 percent of the married people who rated their marriages as unhappy and decided to stay together, rated their marriage as having improved five years later."[3] Stay with us and find out why it is worth not only giving it a try but also building a strong family that will prevail and leave a legacy for future generations.

We strongly believe that this kind of transformation cannot occur by attending a workshop or seminar or reading some articles or books. As educators we strongly believe that real learning and transformation only occur in a well-planned and elaborated process. This process not only has to include teaching but also interaction, assessment, reflection and assimilation, practice and mastery, sharing what has been learned, and reporting to accountability partners or coaches. That is precisely why we developed the Marriage Serious Business University, the online coaching tool that complements this book and that incorporates the latest and most successful trends in learning and behavior transformation. We invest thousands of dollars in our education and careers but most of us overlook our most important investment and endeavor. We never really got the intensive training nor the certification to become a parent or spouse, did we? We should not leave the future of our relationships in the hands of luck or fate. If we want to see real change and progress in our relationships we should consider registering right now and not let this transformation opportunity go by. Go sign up today at www.MarriageSeriousBusiness.com/University

Sincerely yours,
Lawrence Otarola
Charlotte, NC

INTRODUCTION

Songs, poems, movies, books—you name it. It's everywhere. Many believe love is all we need for a successful and truthful relationship, with phrases like "live out of love," or "love is all we need." The truth is, for centuries marriage was regarded as the most important business enterprise of all. Parents decided whom their children would marry, often based on the dowry the "prospect" brought as a sign of commitment, partnership, and long-term purpose. It was the most significant and highest investment someone would make in his or her lifespan. This dowry represented the "initial investment" of the new family business enterprise. Every household was a production unit in and of itself; each family member performed specific duties and tasks to make the family work and prosper. They farmed and processed their goods and used them for their own maintenance or exchanged them for other goods needed. Family and marriage was very serious business.

The sexual revolution of the 1960s, however, shifted the pendulum to the other side: the emotional side. "Keeping the affection ignited and romance alive" has been the mantra ever since. But marriage, as those of us who are married eventually discover, is a lot more than emotions and pep rallies. This shift moved marriage to the other side of the spectrum, and now it is all about sex, romance, and attraction. Has it worked? No, it hasn't. On the contrary, hundreds of children are growing up in homes where the father or mother figure is absent or where two strangers in foster homes are raising them. The divorce rate has increased like never before in the history of humankind. There is an epidemic of single parents, abortions, cheating, and undisciplined children, to say the least. Family conflicts have escalated to alarming levels.

Marriage is serious business. We regard it as the most important investment and endeavor in life. Cultivating a successful marriage benefits spouses, their children, relatives, and entire communities. A good marriage contributes to the well-being of its members in terms of mental and physical health, academic achievement, emotional stability, financial success, and in building a healthy and vibrant society.

According to Robert H. Coombs, "Married people live longer and, in general, are physically and emotionally healthier than those who are not married."[4] He also stated that married people have lower indexes of alcoholism, suicide, and mental health problems than those who are not married.

It is our mission to persuade our generation and subsequent generations that family and marriage mean serious business. To achieve this, we have to go back to the basics. Marriage was built upon the "*Three Foundational Pillars of Marriage, Serious Business*" that hold it together and make it a very serious business.

First Foundational Pillar: A Sense of Commitment

Marriage was established as the first human institution regulated by a mutual commitment to stay together, care for, support, and help each other through thick and thin. Everybody recognizes that the commitment "to have and to hold from this day forward, for better or for worse, for richer, for poorer, in sickness and in health, to love and to cherish" is by far the mark of a marriage relationship. That commitment is made to God, each other, and the fruit of their love, their children.

Second Foundational Pillar: A Sense of Partnership

Why do two people partner in a business? Is it not because one has something the other lacks and vice versa? Likewise, in marriage, man and woman are, in essence, a "complement" to each other, with specific and distinct gifts and abilities. That union is the supreme expression of wholeness, fulfillment, and intimacy. In other words, it is a powerful partnership, identified worldwide by the well-known phrase, "And they will become one flesh."

Third Foundational Pillar: A Sense of Purpose

This new partnership has a mission. That mission can only be accomplished through mutual cooperation. Married couples want to build a home and have children who will become good men and women. This mission brings enormous benefits not only to their families but also to society as a whole. We all have an innate desire for continuity; that desire also prompts us to think about the legacy we want to leave to our future generations. It is the moral responsibility of every couple to build a marriage that surpasses that of their parents, and they have the moral and spiritual responsibility to provide opportunities for their children to surpass them as well. This sense of purpose leads us to think about the benefits of being married and staying together and about the legacy we are leaving behind.

A marriage that operates as a serious business under these foundational pillars does not generally look like the popular model portrayed in mass media (i.e., a father working outside, a mother staying at home, and children impeccably groomed). Obviously, this model is often a distorted image of what marriage really is for many families—perhaps most families. On the contrary, the successful "marriage partnership" is not about establishing and maintaining popular institutional images, but rather purposely implementing principles of universal application, which accommodate the socioeconomic realities of the applicable environment.

Now that we have mentioned some of the benefits of staying married and the foundational pillars that hold marriage together, the million-dollar question is, how can we make it work? We can accomplish our goal by carefully setting up the framework that will allow us to build a solid and durable home. In the following pages, we will argue in favor of embodying in our marriages many of the principles that every successful business takes seriously.

STATE OF
THE BUSINESS

BE AWARE OF
THE RISK SOURCES

*E*very successful business has incorporated a Risk Management policy that allows them to identify, assess, and prioritize the effects of uncertainty in their bottom line. This is accomplished by developing a strategic and economical plan to minimize and control the impact of unfortunate events. The purpose of this Risk Management policy is to ensure that the company will not deviate from its business goals when uncertainty strikes. It is important to note that this uncertainty comes from internal and external risk sources. These risk sources are also tangible and intangible, human and technological. All these sources makes its management extremely difficult to implement.

According to the Institute for Business and Home Safety (IBHS), an estimated 25 percent of businesses do not reopen following a major disaster. You can protect your business by identifying the risks associated with natural and man-made disasters, and by creating a plan for action should a disaster strike. By keeping those plans updated, you can help ensure the survival of your business."[5]

Just as there are risk sources that determine the likelihood of success or failure of any business, there are also a number of sources that can determine the level of risk faced by any marriage. These *"Marriage Partnership Risk Sources"* have been compiled from observations and investigations into the primary causes of divorce. Being aware of these risk sources and determining the degree to which they are present in our relationships can be crucial to better understanding what we are experiencing and, at the same time, measuring the risk that we may be facing in our marriages or future marriages.

It is essential to be aware of the state of your marriage partnership, and to identify the *Risk Sources of Marriage, Serious Business.* It is equally important to learn how to deal with the uncertainty produced by them, and to prepare yourselves to manage and minimize their impact in your present or future marriages. The Rules of the Game are the strategic and systematic process by which we overcome the Risk Sources and build strong and healthy marriages and families.

Risk Source One:

BACKGROUND

*S*everal years ago, my wife and I met a newlywed couple and became pretty close to them. For privacy, let's call them Carlos from Costa Rica and Becky from the United States. One day Becky told my wife how she felt increasingly frustrated every time Carlos left his underwear on the bathroom floor after taking a shower. She finally decided to let it pile up until it captured Carlos's attention. Before jumping to conclusions, we need to understand that Carlos grew up as a single child, and his mother spoiled him in every way possible. Carlos was raised believing that it was somebody else's responsibility to pick up his clothes.

We all grew up in different environments with different beliefs and habits. Sometimes cultural values and norms affect the way we perceive what should be normal and acceptable. We call the sum of our formative experiences, values, and perceptions our "background." Each of us has different backgrounds that can range from similar to extremely opposite, and certain elements of our backgrounds may create sources of conflict. Therefore, our backgrounds constitute our Risk Source One. It is essential that we understand how this source can affect and determine the degree of success or failure in marriage.

According to David Popenoe, "People who are similar in their values, backgrounds, and life goals are more likely to have a successful marriage. Opposites may attract, but they may not live together harmoniously as married couples. People who share common backgrounds and similar social networks are better suited as marriage partners than people who are very different in their backgrounds and networks."[6] There are couples who, like Carlos and Becky, come from very different backgrounds. Some come from cultures and countries with very different values and worldviews about family, life purpose, conventions, and even hygienic practices. Others are from the same countries and cultures but with very different family customs and values.

There are certain questions that can help us understand if the background gap between our spouses and ourselves might pose additional risk to our marriages or future marriages. We should think carefully about the following questions: Do my marriage partner and I come from countries and cultures that are very similar or very different? Does my spouse or fiancé come from a family with customs and values very similar or very different to mine? If we come from similar cultures or families, our level of risk is lower. Marriage is already hard, having gaps like this one can create additional conflicts that might add some degree of conflict and uncertainty in our home. Once again, our answers would help us determine our level of risk.

This risk source should be a conversation starter, something to think and talk about, to evaluate, and to measure the degree in which it may or may not be affecting us as marriage partners. In the following chapter we will be talking about our parents' marriage. Have you ever wondered how their mistakes and flaws may or may not impact our relationship today?

Risk Source Two:

MARRIAGE OF OUR PARENTS

his risk source can impair the functioning and survival of our marriages. Today, it is accepted that a combination of genetic and environmental forces uniquely shapes our personality traits. The first five years of our lives are crucial in molding our values, characters, and worldviews. We get our core values and first impressions of marriage and parenthood from home.

Looking back on how my parents lived out their marriage, I now realize they had severe impairments in several areas. There are some good memories about them as parents, but, concerning their marriage, I cannot remember my parents hugging or kissing except the imposed family tradition of kissing upon leaving or returning. I remember my dad becoming mad if my mother, my brother, or I would not give him a kiss in greeting. I also cannot remember my parents engaging in a conversation where laughing and cuddling was involved or solving their differences in an effective and successful way.

What I can clearly remember is the tension created every time my dad put my mom down, inside and outside of our home, or when he drove back home zigzagging because he was drunk. I can remember my dad stopping at a bar and making us wait for hours in the car. I can remember my mother, in her desperation, flirting with other men every single opportunity she had. I also remember her taking us in the car to get in touch with the man that later became her second husband. I can remember the endless fights while I was in bed trying to get some sleep to go to school the next day. I can remember my mother complaining that my dad was not providing enough and my dad accusing her of not knowing how to manage their budget. To make a long story short, my parents divorced when I was ten.

There are certain questions that can give us insight and help us understand whether the kind of life and marriage our parents had could pose a serious risk to us today. For example, are my parents or the parents of my spouse divorced? If we respond by saying that we come from a stable home where our parents have remained together over the years, faced and dodged the problems and difficulties of life, and stayed united throughout their marriage, our level of risk is lower. But if we respond that we are the products of divorced parents, then studies show that we have a greater chance of suffering the same fate as our parents if we don't correct the mistakes that our parents made.

The following research states, "Children of divorce have a higher risk of divorce when they marry and an even higher risk if the person they marry comes from a divorced home. One study found that when the wife alone had experienced a parental divorce, her odds of divorce increased to 59 percent. When both spouses experienced parental divorce, the odds of divorce nearly tripled to 189 percent."[7]

Have you noticed that the older we become, the more we look like our parents? Whether it's good or bad, their values and behavior patterns have been carved into our minds and hearts.

Another question to ponder is, did my parents communicate with ease or with difficulty? We can agree that if our parents communicated with ease, our level of risk is lower. However, if we say that they hardly agreed on anything and were always complaining that their partner never understood them, then we have a higher risk for further conflict and frustration, which can destabilize our homes because, in most cases, we copy the behavioral patterns and responses our parents have modeled for us.

We also need to ponder the following questions—each question should be answered by both partners:

- Did my parents resolve their problems easily or with difficulty?
- Did my parents express love, affection, and physical contact often or rarely to never?
- Did my parents physically and emotionally assault each other and, if so, how frequently?
- Did my parents' siblings avoid divorce, or was divorce common?
- Did my parents come from a home where their brothers and sisters had problems with alcohol and drugs?
- Does my mother come from a matriarchy where wives control and decide family matters; or did she come from a home where both parents worked together, talked, and decided things as a team?
- Was my father a product of "macho" conditioning, used to having the last word in all matters and looking to be served at all times; or did he come from a home where household members had the right and freedom to express their opinions and be part of the decision making?

Answering these questions with an open heart and mind can help us identify the areas in which we might have some issues, not just to be aware of these problems but most importantly, to change the direction of our stories.

Surely, based on my parents' marriage, the odds were not on my side. My wife, on the other hand, witnessed a mother who literally sacrificed herself for her children. However, she never displayed any care, affection, or romantic expression for her husband. My wife and I are still married after almost thirty years, but don't get me wrong. It has not been an easy ride for us. We have had many bumps, steep paths, and deadly curves that have been overcome by our strong conviction that marriage is a long-term investment—one that will produce its best fruits and benefits if we decide to persevere, invest, work hard, and are determined to make it work. We strongly believe that marriage is very serious business. However, we also believe that the best is ahead of us.

Now, let me be honest. Have we overcome everything? No, there are still many things we do not yet know how to make work, solve, and overcome. But for us, as good marriage entrepreneurs, the important thing is to look back and see where we are now, remembering where we came from, and looking ahead to where we are determined to go. We have experienced firsthand the effects of our parents' marriages on our perceptions and behavioral patterns. Knowing the impact this risk source has had in our marriage, we have decided to take precautionary steps to address, as much as possible, these behavioral patterns every time they surge.

One thing must be clear: we refuse to use our parent's background as an excuse or as a sentence of our fate. Therefore, we should be talking about the degree in which this risk source may or may not be affecting us as marriage partners. We already talked about our background and the kind of marriage our parents had.

As we continue with other risk sources, have you ever wondered how our past relationships may or may not affect us? Is the past really behind us?

Risk Source Three:
PAST RELATIONSHIPS

*E*zra and Elizabeth got married several years ago with great dreams and aspirations. Even though Elizabeth came from a very conflicted childhood, Ezra was in love and didn't consider it important. As a teen, Elizabeth went through a wild phase of sexual activity. However, in Ezra she finally found someone to love and be loved by. She was excited and happy! After a few years, Ezra started feeling that what happened to Elizabeth was not just part of the past but a part of the present, and it was affecting both Elizabeth and him. The bill was passed to him, and he was paying overprice for it. After several separations, counseling, and family and pastoral intervention, they finally divorced.

Even when we hide our pasts or believe the past doesn't have anything to do with our present, according to the following research, past relationships may affect our current and future relationships—especially our past, sexually active relationships (whether dating, cohabitation, or marriage). There are significant physical consequences, but there are also remarkable emotional and psychological effects that may impact subsequent relationships.

According to David Popenoe, "People who have multiple cohabiting relationships before marriage are more likely to experience marital conflict, marital unhappiness, and eventual divorce than people who do not cohabit before marriage. Researchers attribute some, but not all, of these differences to the characteristics of people who cohabit, the so-called 'selection effect,' rather than to the experience of cohabiting itself. It has been suggested that the negative effects of cohabitation on future marital success may diminish as living together becomes a common experience. However, according to one study of couples who were married between 1981 and 1997, the negative effects persist among younger cohorts, supporting the view that the cohabitation experience itself contributes to problems in marriage."[8]

As we can see from the above-mentioned research, those past relationships can destabilize our marriages. In many cases, emotional, spiritual, physical, and psychological scars might emerge, many times disguised as guilt or isolation. All of this "junk" we carry from the past can prevent us from developing one of the *"Main Key Ingredients of Marriage, Serious Business"* for success in marriage going forward: *intimacy* that results from building healthy transparency and accountability between spouses.

There are certain questions we need to carefully ponder that might help us find out whether past relationships in which we were sexually active pose a serious risk to us today. Do thoughts assail us or prompt us to remember those past relationships? Do we tend to compare our husbands or wives with partners that we had in the past? Does guilt prevent us from giving ourselves entirely to our spouse, thus affecting our *intimacy*?

We must respond thoroughly to each of these questions to get a better idea of the danger our marriage may be in. Even more, we should be talking with a qualified professional about how this risk source may or may not have affected us and how it could be impacting us as marriage partners or future marriage partners.

We already talked about our background, the kind of marriage our parents had, and the way our past relationships might impact us. Sadly, there is another risk source we should be taking into consideration that might affect our relationship. This is precisely what we are about to talk next, how our religion or faith may or may not affect our relationships. Aren't you wondering how a good thing such as faith can turn into something negative?

Risk Source Four:

RELIGION

arion and Valerie got married in spite of the opposition shown by both families because of their religious backgrounds. Marion was an evangelical Protestant, and Valerie was Jewish. They were in love, and with a Shakespearean idea of love, thought their different religious backgrounds would not be an issue. Marion asked Valerie, "What if we go to your synagogue on Saturday and on Sunday, we go to my church?" Valerie thought that was a great idea. However, the first problems arose when, after church, they started talking about the messages or rituals in each other's place of worship. After several months, a sense of resentment and resistance developed as a result of the prolonged and repeated disputes about the matter. Eventually they agreed to go separately.

When their kids entered the picture, Valerie's maternal instinct grew stronger, and she refused to allow Marion to take the kids to his church. She wanted them to be devoted Jews, just as she was. The struggle continued for years, and when the kids grew up and embarked on their own lives, Marion and Valerie got divorced. It is important to point out that my wife and I are not implying that all interfaith couples would end up like this.

However, how can a good thing become a risk source in marriage? Well, one of the realities of life is that humans have an amazing ability to turn good things into bad things. The issue here is not that religion is bad or good or that one is better than the other—we refer to a marriage where each partner has a different religion. We all know that religion plays an important role in the lives of most people. So much so, that for years many people have been saying that there are three topics we should never bring to the table: politics, sports, and religion. Why? Because talking about religion can start a fiery conflict, figuratively leading us all into World War III. When a husband or wife practices a religion other than the one his or her partner practices, a number of additional discussions can manifest that would not have occurred if that religious difference did not exist.

We need to ponder some very important questions that can help us understand whether or not religion is a risk source in our relationships. We could mention a number of "holy issues" that could bring additional friction and difficulties in a marriage. For example, should we baptize our children when they are infants? Should they wear religious attire? Should we participate in each other's family's religious occasions or holidays? As far as faith is concerned, do my partner and I have completely different faiths? The list is endless. We are more likely to have additional conflicts since, in most cases, differences in faith can affect our home. These fundamental differences might bring constant disagreement not only between the couple but also between their families as well.

We should ask ourselves another key question that can make a big difference: Is my partner open-minded and caring toward my religious beliefs or very narrow-minded and stubborn? This basic characteristic will make a difference in the degree of conflict and problems that can arise from having different faiths. If the husband or wife is open and understanding, the degree of conflict that may arise will obviously be less. But if the husband or wife is very narrow-minded and intransigent, "faith" can become a living hell at home. When it comes to faith, spouses can accomplish more by speaking louder with their lives than with their mouths. Therefore, we should be talking about how this risk source may or may not be affecting us as marriage partners.

We already talked about our background, the kind of marriage our parents had, the way our past relationships might impact us, and how our religion or faith might also become an issue. Have you ever wonder how our finances may or may not affect us? We all know that money is not the most important thing in life but we will see next how excruciating it might become?

Risk Source Five:

FINANCES

*T*here is a popular saying, "Money is not everything, but it helps." In most cases, things can go very well until financial problems arise. Someone jokingly suggested to me that on the wedding day, the minister should say, "Till debt do us part." Another story goes that there was once a man who was robbed at gunpoint, and the robber threatened him by saying, "Your money or your life?" To that, the man replied bitterly, "What money? What life? Can't you see I am married?"

We all know that finances play an important role in the lives of every family. So much that countless jokes are made about men who are not good prospects because they don't have anything to offer a woman financially; they are not "marriage material." A friend of mine used to say that she wanted to marry a man with "good feelings," and while saying that, she moved her fingers, signaling money. Then she added, "He must also have a good heart," moving her hands like someone driving a large luxury vehicle.

Economic changes and financial issues have profound effects on marriage because they reach the core of every *"Husband and Wife's Fundamental Needs of Marriage, Serious Business."* Wives have a fundamental need for *stability and security.* This need is directly threatened at a time of financial crisis. Wives often turn against their husbands and begin to question their ability and willingness to be a provider and caregiver. This leads to a decreased level of admiration and respect that they have for their husbands.

The perceived loss of *admiration and respect* can affect husbands, who have a fundamental need for both. This need is directly threatened in a financial crisis because the levels of admiration and respect from their wives reach critical levels. The issue deepens when the husband's self-esteem declines—when they think that there is something wrong with them, due to not being able to provide or take care of their spouses and children. This is the fundamental reason why financial crises hit both husbands and wives deeply. In fact, this is one of the nine risk sources that critically affects married couples and often leads marriages to fail.

There are certain questions that can point us in the right direction, helping us understand whether our current financial condition represents a danger or risk source in the home. Sit down with your marriage partner or fiancé and ponder this question: Who provides the highest financial contribution to the household? For some husbands, when their wives contribute a larger portion of income, they may feel threatened and belittled. On the other hand, some wives in that position may underestimate the role of their husbands at home, affecting their husband's need for admiration and respect, often pointing out who contributes the most. In that case they might be more likely to have additional problems. If we answer that we are that kind of spouses or fiancés, our level of risk could be higher than saying that we don't care who brings home the higher income.

Another key question is: Do I have confidence in the way my partner handles our finances? This question hits a key nerve in marriage. Marriage is a partnership, and its main asset is love. One of the main by-products of love is trust. If husbands or wives do not trust the way their partner handles the finances, conflict could arise between the two partners.

Another key question is whether we allow our partners to be aware of how we spend our money and whether we are willing to be accountable. Just imagine a business that does not have a common fund, where each department does as they please and spends money without any accountability. That is why it is essential for a business to have a common budget. Its funds may be budgeted in different accounts for different things, but a key aspect of a business is to have commonality. In the same fashion, marriage must have commonality. Each spouse might have his or her own savings account for contingencies or personal expenses, but it is key to have a common family budget. We must take these questions seriously if we want to get a better idea of the level of risk our marriages might be facing when it comes to managing our finances. Equally important, we should be talking about how this risk source may or may not be affecting us as marriage partners.

We spoke on background; the kind of marriage our parents had; the way our past relationships might impact us; how our religion or faith might also become an issue; and how our finances might really be a thorn in the flesh. As the list of risk sources grow, we can see that these sources can jeopardize our marriage partnership.

We should be taking into consideration how age may be another risk source and how it may or may not affect us. We should ask ourselves, "Is there an age in which it is better to get married?" We have all heard that age is not an important factor in love. But is that an accurate statement?

Risk Source Six:

AGE

ome very dear friends of ours had a son, Allan, who was still single at age forty-five. He was a great son, responsible and independent. When Maria met Allan, she went after him relentlessly. She was the kind of woman who doesn't accept "no" for an answer. Our friends were very concerned, not only because Maria was the one making all the decisions in the relationship, but also because she was sixty-five at the time. They talked to Allan several times trying to point out the possible consequences their age difference might bring to his life.

Maria and Allan got married in spite of friends' and relatives' concerns. My friends supported Allan and tried to give them the space the new couple needed. However, in less than a year Allan came back with the news that he had divorced. "It didn't work, Dad," Allan said. "I couldn't stand it any longer." My wife and I are not trying to imply that marriages with an age difference never work. What we are stating here is that age does matter, and it brings additional elements that can pose areas of conflict and risk.

Mainstream entertainment portrays the romantic idea that in love, age doesn't matter. However, studies show that, in general, age is a factor that can negatively affect relationships. Once the age differences become more evident, in many instances the older person starts to watch over his or her younger partner very closely, and the younger person starts experiencing a sharp decrease in physical attraction toward his or her partner.

We have also observed that, when it comes to age, there is a *"Best Window of Time of Marriage, Serious Business"* in which marriage is most likely to succeed. It seems that very early in life, marriage can bring unbearable emotional and financial burdens for the couple. Likewise, later in life people have greater difficulty adjusting and renouncing their adult habits. Various sources support the idea of this window. For example, one study suggests that a window exists for women between ages eighteen and twenty-five. "Fifty-nine percent of marriages for women under the age of eighteen end in divorce within fifteen years. The divorce rate drops to 36 percent for those married at age twenty or older."[9] Another study states that "50 percent of all marriages in which the brides are twenty-five or older result in a failed marriage."[10]

These studies suggest that there is a window in a woman's life between eighteen and twenty-five in which marriage has a higher chance of success.

These two conditions can bring serious problems to marriage, and sooner or later it can wear down life's most important investment and endeavor. But certain questions can point us in the right direction and help us ponder whether age is a risk source in our relationships or not. For example, were we under age twenty or over age thirty when we married? Or, are we going to be married? If the answer is that we were younger than twenty, we'll most likely experience greater problems because we likely lack the financial preparation or maturity for such a serious life project. If the answer is that we were over thirty years old, we'll most likely experience greater problems adjusting and letting go of established habits and ideas about ourselves and our lifestyles—the way things should be and how the relationship should work.

Adult habits and routines are formed and entrenched in our twenties. When people marry during those years, they develop adult habits and routines together. In contrast, if people wait beyond that window of time, they will develop these habits individually, eventually hindering the process of adapting to their partners with ease.

Marriage is a partnership that requires intimate knowledge of our partners that takes time and willingness to expose, simply because it puts us in a position of vulnerability. It seems that it is easier to open up more freely in our early adult years. We must be able to respond to the questions previously asked in order to better understand the risk level we might have in our marriage partnership in regards to age differences or window of opportunity. We should be talking about how this risk source could affect us, or even our children, younger relatives, or friends that are about to take that important step in life.

We already talked about our background, the kind of marriage our parents had, the way our past relationships might have impacted us, how our religion or faith might also become an issue, how our finances might really be the thorn in the flesh, and how the age factor could have impacted us or others we care about.

Adding to these risk sources, we will talk about how important it is to have a support network around us, and how the lack of it might put us at a higher risk. We all know how important it is to have someone to talk to when things go wrong. Shouldn't we all have a shoulder to cry on or a hand to hold during those difficult times?

SUPPORT NETWORK

*M*y wife is the youngest of eight brothers and sisters. She was born when her mother was forty-five and her dad was fifty-six. She was only thirteen when she lost her mother and was pretty much left on her own during her crucial years. When all of her brothers and sisters had families of their own, she found in one sister and one brother the necessary support to make it through for a couple of years until their own spouses considered her a pebble in their shoes. Finding herself with no way out and nowhere to go, her pastor and his wife took her in as their own child.

It wasn't that different for me. My mother remarried shortly after her divorce. My father refused to give up and fought his way out of his pain legally, forcing my brother and me to testify in court against our own mother. When the emotions receded a little bit, my parents, engaged in their own affairs, never really involved themselves in our lives. Even so, my parents wholeheartedly tried to do their best in spite of the circumstances they had faced.

Even when we did not have the support network in our family to help us through, we found older couples in our church that provided direction and support for us. My wife and I still remember very vividly some of the expressions they taught us, like, "Never stop going on dates," or "Never go to bed without resolving an argument," or "Learn to live within your limits." They not only provided good counsel but also companionship in times of difficulty and trial.

David Popenoe states, "Despite the romantic notion that people meet and fall in love through chance or fate, evidence suggests that social networks are important in bringing together individuals of similar interests and backgrounds. According to a large-scale national survey, almost 60 percent of married people were introduced by family, friends, co-workers, or other acquaintances."[11] There's an old Hebrew adage that says, "Better a nearby friend than a distant relative." This speaks of the importance of receiving support at times of one's greatest need. How important is having someone on our side when most needed!

When it comes to marriage, a *"Support Network of Marriage, Serious Business"* made up of people who have been together over the years, despite the difficulties and hardships of life is essential to the success of the marriage partnership. We're not talking about a perfect marriage—there is no such thing—but those partners in a marriage who, in spite of their differences and limitations, have decided to persevere because there is a greater purpose, one that brings major benefits in the long term. By this we mean a successful marriage partnership. As we can see from the studies we are citing, couples who stay married surpass, in all measures, those who are divorced, living together, or are single.

Of course, much depends on the quality of the support network around us. What if we have friends telling us, "Leave that woman; she is dragging you down" or "I told you! Leave that animal; he is a beast! If he sneaks around, you pay him back twice as hard so he learns his lesson and realizes who he is dealing with."

Advice like this may sound very tempting at first, but in the end it will more likely help kill the marriage. Unfortunately, many of our friends have neither the skills nor the attitudes necessary to build a solid home; that is, a successful marriage partnership. The absence or presence of this source is key to our success or failure. We must keep this in mind because if we have a support group around us, it can be a valuable asset for our life's most important investment and endeavor.

Certain questions can help us determine whether we really have a support network around our marriages. For instance, "When we were getting married or about to get married, what was the attitude of our family toward the person we were marrying?" If the answer is that the family opposed the marriage and disagreed, it is likely that we do not have the kind of support needed to face the ups and downs that every marriage goes through during its formative years. If the answer is that the family supported the marriage and agreed, we likely have helping hands; people who will listen and provide wise counsel in times of uncertainty and confusion.

The same is true of our close circle of friends; what was the attitude of our friends when they learned that we were getting married? If the answer is that our friends opposed the marriage and disagreed, we likely do not have the support that friends can provide in tough times; they will easily say, "I told you so." If the answer is that our friends supported the marriage and agreed, it is likely we have the kind of support, intimacy, and trust that only a network of close friends can provide. We must respond seriously to each of these questions to get a better idea of the level of risk we might have in our marriages if we lack the proper kind of support network. Not only that, but we should even be talking about how this risk source may have affected us or might affect us in the future.

We already talked about our background, the kind of marriage our parents had, the way our past relationships might have impacted us, how our religion or faith might also become an issue, how our finances might really be the thorn in the flesh, how the age factor could have impacted us or others we care about, and about the importance of having a support network around us to go to not only in those difficult seasons of life but at any time. What other risk source should we be taking into consideration that might impact our relationship?

If you think that is enough, I have news for you; there is still more. Next we will be talking about how those seasons of change in our lives can put us in such a hot spot, a very vulnerable one. We all know how difficult those seasons of change are but how that can impact our relationships goes beyond our imagination. Do you have any idea to what degree?

PERIOD OF CHANGE

he business philosopher Peter F. Drucker said, "Everybody has accepted by now that change is unavoidable. But that still implies that change is like death and taxes; it should be postponed as long as possible and no change would be vastly preferable. But in a period of upheaval, such as the one we are living in, change is the norm."[12] When it comes to marriage, change is not only inevitable but the norm. Life throws us curves, and we need to learn how to deal with them. However, the problem is not change but how we react to it.

If there has been a constant in our marriage, it is change. Right after we got married, we moved from Costa Rica to Argentina to pursue our studies. Even though our stay in Argentina was a little less than a year, the cultural shock and exposure to a large variety of peoples from all over the continent provided us with the skills we needed for the years to come. That period of time was followed by six years of apparent stability, if you consider the births of three children such a thing. However, after that period a new change was ahead of us: an invitation to come work in the United States.

We had to start all over again—new friends, new neighbors, new schools, new jobs, new culture and language. The adaptation process wasn't easy, and just when we thought we were starting to settle down, Hurricane Floyd crossed our path, producing the third largest evacuation in US history; over 2.5 million residents in the East Coast were ordered to evacuate their homes. Our house flooded over four-and-a-half feet, and it remained flooded for an entire week, producing radical and inconvenient change in our lives.

Two years after that, when our oldest son was going into ninth grade, our middle son into seventh grade, and our daughter into third grade, we moved to Charlotte, North Carolina, and started all over again. That very same year of change, we faced our most difficult trial up to that time. One of our kids was diagnosed with a neurological condition that drastically changed our lives forever. A short time after this, my wife's sister, who happens to be her best friend as well, lost her husband who was killed in a car theft. A few more years passed, and her sister lost her twenty-one-year-old daughter to heart failure. And, if all these events were not enough change, the economic world crisis of 2008 left my wife and I unemployed, producing additional stress and difficulties in our lives. In that same period, my dad at just 70, passed away.

Marriages that go through a period of change are more vulnerable and more likely to fail. We should understand and be attentive to the possible risks involved when we go through seasons of change in our lives. There are certain questions that might raise a flag and reveal whether the changes we are going through might put our marriages at a higher risk. For instance, "Have we moved recently?" Do we move often? Is one or more of our close relatives facing serious illness? Up to now, have any relatives or loved ones recently passed away? Am I living a nightmare at work? Am I experiencing prolonged unemployment? If we respond to any of these questions affirmatively, we are at a higher risk.

To get a better idea of the levels of risk we might be facing in our marriage, we must respond thoroughly to each of these questions, building up defenses around our marriages against those vulnerabilities. No matter what, we have to make it through; we can't just give up! And that is precisely the reason why we should be talking about how this risk source may be affecting us right now or in the future.

We already talked about our background, the kind of marriage our parents had, the way our past relationships might have impacted us, how our religion or faith might also become an issue, how our finances might really be the thorn in the flesh, how the age factor might impact us or is affecting others we care about, the importance of having a support network around us to go to not only in those difficult seasons of life but at any time, and how those seasons of change might hit us pretty badly, leaving us at the brink of divorce. Many of us don't realize how so many risk sources are impacting our relationships and families in such drastic or subtle ways.

There is one more risk source we will be talking about; one that has to do with how we get along with each other. We all have heard the expression, "There is some chemistry between us." What level of compatibility is there in our relationship, are there different platforms of compatibility? How can these *Compatibility Platforms of Marriage, Serious Business* affect us one way or the other?

Risk Source Nine:

COMPATIBILITY

*J*ustin Rosenstein said, "Working together in concert more smoothly not only helps us move more quickly, it changes the nature of what we can undertake. When we have the confidence that we can orchestrate the group effort required to realize them, we dare bigger dreams."[13]

Compatibility is more than "uniformity"; it is more than "chemistry." One way of explaining compatibility is by comparing it to a puzzle: each piece of a puzzle fits only with the right piece. Compatibility is not about perfection; it's about complementation. In other words, compatibility maximizes the strengths of the parties involved, while lack of compatibility hinders and wears them out. Compatibility brings out the best in people, helping create the best version of us. Couples who have personality traits that complement each other are more likely to stay together than those who are incompatible in almost every personality trait measured.

We would like to introduce to you the three *"Compatibility Platforms of Marriage, Serious Business."* The first platform of compatibility is the *"Personality Platform."* At this level we want to make sure that even when there is "chemistry" between the two, we have personalities that are compatible. There are hundreds of tools to measure our personality compatibility. We would like to suggest a question that can give us insight about the issue. One question for the first platform could be, "Do my partner and I have personalities that complement each other, or do we frequently feel frustrated and disappointed with each other?" Xinia and I love each other deeply. However, we have very little compatibility at a personality level. When we got married we didn't have the tools to measure our compatibility. It has not been easy for us to make it work but we have not given up because we know that we have to overcome these differences for a greater good, a greater purpose; the benefit of our marriage partnership, our most important investment and endeavor.

The second platform of compatibility is the *"Values Platform."* Even when we experience a high degree of compatibility at a personality level, if we have very different values about family and marriage, our relationships will face very serious problems. At this level, we want to make sure that we both share common values, especially when it comes to marriage. For example, "Am I experiencing a manageable or unsolvable disagreement with my partner over the handling of finances at home?" or "Am I experiencing a manageable or unsolvable disagreement with my partner regarding how we discipline our children?" If the answer is that we have unsolvable disagreements, then this is evidence of a conflict of values and places us at higher risk. It is at this platform that my wife and I share the strongest compatibility. We have very similar values in all spheres of life, especially when it comes to what is important to us in life, and we both value our family and marriage.

The third platform of compatibility is the *"Life Purpose Platform."* At this level, we want to make sure that in the long run we will still be walking side by side. There are many couples who disregard this key platform and marry someone they honestly and passionately love, only to later regret not having followed their "life call" when, over the years, the middle-age crisis comes, and they can begin feeling like they have put aside their "life purpose" for the sake of staying with their spouses. Many marriages end twenty, thirty, even forty years later because one of the marriage partners decides to go after their "life dream." Here again, my wife and I are united by a very strong and common sense of life purpose. This life purpose has been the glue that has kept us together throughout these three decades.

As you can see, being aware of the risk sources is essential to helping us identify what our vulnerable areas are and place our energy and effort in building the necessary fences to manage our weaknesses. However, this only helps us adopt a defensive mode against the risk sources that can undermine our marriage partnerships. As vital as that can be, awareness alone cannot give us the clarity and tools to be successful. As we mentioned before, just as nine out of ten entrepreneurs who know the Rules of the Game will succeed, in the same fashion, those couples who know and put into action the Rules of the Game for marriage will not only flourish but will also be on the offensive, achieve great success, fulfillment, and leave a legacy for future generations. In the following pages, we will address the first Rule of the Game that will help you set the cornerstone of a stronger and long-lasting relationship.

RULES OF
THE GAME

Rule of the Game One:
REGARD MARRIAGE AS A ONE-OF-A-KIND CONTRACT

Objective
That each marriage partner understand that, just as a contract protects and regulates the capital and function of any serious business, marriage is protected and regulated by a legal and moral contract.

Contractual Relationship
- An agreement between two or more parties that bonds them together for a determined purpose or mission and that specifies acceptable or unacceptable behavior from the parties involved.
- An agreement enforceable by law.
- The formal agreement of marriage: betrothal.

Note for our Christian readers:

Why contract and not covenant? Among Christian circles this topic seems to be a controversial issue. Amid such dispute, there is one thing that is a fact: The use of both Greek and Hebrew terms for contract or covenant is the same. It was used indistinctly for sacred purposes as well as commercial day-to-day agreements. Although we decided to use the term contract to reach a mainstream audience, we have not diminished the seriousness of marriage, on the contrary, when we intentionally call it a "One-of-a-Kind Contract" we are making it a synonym of "Covenant" by emphasizing its uniqueness and sacredness, as you will see in the following pages.

Marriage Case Study

Amanda and Jake have decided to move in together, as many couples do today. They believe that love doesn't need to be regulated by a "piece of paper." Amanda's parents are the result of the sexual revolution of the '60s and have been very lenient with her.

"Sweetie," said her mother, "it would be better for you to try and experience all you can before getting married, than to have regrets later."

Amanda is the kind of girl that is very open-minded, modern, and self-confident. She is also the kind of woman who would never allow any man to take advantage of her.

"Don't try to control me or take advantage of me," she told Jake, "because the day you try it, you will never see me again."

On the other hand, Jake's parents are old-fashioned. Having their son move in with Amanda on a trial basis upsets them. Even though Jake's mother is convinced that marriage is beneficial in many ways, she didn't successfully convey those values to her son.

"Son," said Jake's mother, "do what is right for your children and your own well-being, and don't go with the flow."

"Mother," replied an agitated Jake, "marriage is old-fashioned; it doesn't work anymore. We are living in different times now. This is how it is done today. It's better like this—no marriage. And we are saving a lot of money that would otherwise be wasted on a ridiculous wedding. After all, all of our friends recognize that we are already a couple."

For Jake and Amanda, the first months under the same roof are fantastic, with the exception of those uncomfortable moments when they meet with relatives and family friends who ask if they are married.

"I don't know," said Amanda, "I feel weird having to give explanations about our relationship; explaining that we are not married, just living together. Don't you feel the same way?"

"Yeah," Jake agreed in a frustrated and tiresome tone. "Is there a word to call couples living together who are not married?"

"Yes," Amanda replied, "cohabitants, but I don't like that term at all."

"I don't like it either," said Jake.

Main Topic

Just as Amanda and Jake don't see the need for a formal paper to determine the level of love and commitment they have for each other, many couples today do not understand that it is not just about a piece of paper, but rather the binding commitment behind such agreement. Throughout history, humans have regulated their relationships through contracts. Regardless of the scope of those relationships, whether between kingdoms, between buyers and sellers, or between husbands and wives, the contract is often a legal instrument that protects and safeguards those relationships.

Contracts have taken many forms; they have been written, verbal, and symbolic. In the past they were performed by cutting an animal down the middle; or taking off a sandal and giving it to the other party as a symbol of commitment; or putting a wax seal on a written document. The essence of a contract is not in the modality, but in the character and word of the parties involved.

There are people who will do their part, regardless of whether it is written down on paper in the form of a contract. There are others who will not deliver, even if they have signed a paper or split an animal in half as a sign of their seriousness and solemnity toward their agreement. No pledge, split animal, or signed paper can prevent people from failing to deliver what they have promised. The purpose of a contract is not to prevent people from failing, but to determine the consequences when they fail to comply with the agreement. In this book we present a series of rules that constitute the cornerstones of the marriage partnership. The first Rule of the Game is to regard marriage as a one-of-a-kind contract. What does regarding marriage as a one-of-a-kind contract mean?

In every country there exists "incorporated" and "black market" businesses. Black market businesses are outlawed organizations that operate as regular businesses. Incorporated businesses are those established under the law through a legal process and are given a unique identity; that is "incorporated." Many black market businesses actually desire to have all the benefits and rights that incorporated companies have. However, I do not think black market business owners are planning to protest in front of the courts any time soon, arguing that it is not fair that they are not granted the same rights. "It's just a legal technicality," their owners might say, "A simple paper granted from the Department of State should not decide our right to operate as a business." This argument before any legitimate judicial authority will not stand.

In the same fashion, there are those who wish to have the same privileges granted to marriages but are unwilling to assume the level of commitment and formality that marriage demands.

Any serious business that has more than one partner is regulated by a contract that esteems and guarantees the relationship between partners. However, as we will see, a contract is more than a "piece" of paper. A contract expresses the good intentions of the parties involved. There is a popular saying, "He who owes nothing, fears nothing."

A Contract Reveals the Real Intentions of a Person

When you are decided on something and are serious in pursuing what you have set in your heart, there should be no reason to fear signing a document that simply puts in writing what you have already determined in your heart to accomplish. Pat and Alicia have a great business concept and find out they need each other to make it happen. Alicia suggests Pat, "Great, I think we are ready to move on. Let's go ahead and sign a contract that will regulate our business relationship." Pat, bewildered by such a proposition, replies, "I don't believe a piece of paper should regulate our friendship and relationship. Let's just go ahead and do business together." What an insane suggestion from Pat. What savvy and wise businessperson would enter into any serious business without a clear and well-detailed contract?

A contract is simply a written expression of what we claim with our mouths. The first and most important sign of goodwill from a person who wants to do business with another is the willingness to sign a contract regulating the relationship. That sign is the initial step of trust in what could be a lasting business relationship. After all, one does not start a business with the intention of bankrupting it in a couple of years. One starts a business wanting to establish a solid and growing organization that will last for many generations. How different would it have been for Pat and Alicia if Pat had instead replied, "Sure, this is great; where do I need to sign?"

In the same fashion, marriage is a lifelong undertaking. Don't you think that the least we can ask from the person we will give all of our life, body, and soul, is to give us a sign of their goodwill? The best sign of goodwill from a partner is his or her willingness to enter into a relationship seriously and according to the law. Upon legally entering the threshold of marriage, our partners demonstrate that they are truly determined to embark on a solid and permanent marriage partnership.

Although this is not a guarantee of success, this type of gesture speaks volumes about the person's real intentions. By avoiding signing our names on a mere piece of paper, it is as if we are going into a game as if we had already lost. If I feared the outcome of a situation, then I would have second thoughts about it. However, if I were positive about my resolve, then there is nothing to fear by inscribing my signature on a paper.

In business, it is often the case that smaller companies, when put in a position of competition against big corporations, concede the business before they begin. Why? Because they allow themselves to become intimidated and therefore confront their competition with a loser's mentality. Similarly, many couples enter marriage with the same loser's mentality. "Let's try it out first! Let's live together to see if it will work, just in case things don't go well." These couples are unaware that their own words and attitudes are most likely condemning their relationships to failure before they have an opportunity to succeed.

A Contract Regulates and Establishes the Conditions of the Contractual Relationship

Once we are decided on something and want to see it become a reality, we must set everything straight. If we are savvy businesspeople, we'll never partner with someone without being concise about both parties' expectations and "rules" that regulate the relationship. Businesspeople who follow these principles will rarely be surprised by the unexpected that could destroy their dreams and push away their customers.

Likewise in marriage, it is important that the terms and conditions pertaining to the each partner are established clearly from the beginning, especially those that each partner expects from the other. It is essential that both parties understand and agree to the rules that are going to define their relationship. These rules are what we call, the Rules of the Game.

For cohabitants like Amanda and Jake, it is just a matter of being together, enjoying each other in the now; the rest doesn't matter. In a wedding ceremony, you see a delighted bride and a proud groom, surrounded by laughter, music, and all kinds of celebrations. However, they share something in common: most of them have not been taught the Rules of the Game; even worse, they have no idea there is such a thing.

A Contract Provides a Safe Haven

Another reason why there should be a contract is because the people involved guarantee themselves the security of a safe haven in the eyes of the law and their communities. A contract also gives legitimacy to the relationship; it gives you a place and identity before the law and the community. When vendors seek to establish business relationships with other companies, one of the first things they will do is a background check. This usually includes verification that those businesses are registered before the law and are operating with a valid business license. Possession of a current business license gives a sense of legality and seriousness to those who want to ensure the safety of their investment and assets.

In the same way, marriage is a public act that gives legality to a relationship and guarantees a privileged place in society. Cohabiting is recognized by the law in many countries; however, most people who engage in cohabitation do so with the idea that the relationship might be transitory. This temporality is probably the reason why society does not regard cohabitation with the same weight that it regards a more committed relationship, such as a marriage.

A Contract Protects Stakeholders from Breaches in Clauses

There are many stories of people who have launched business ventures with big dreams and high expectations only to soon enter a hellish nightmare. They trusted their partner's good intentions, and eventually ended up being terribly cheated due to a lack of legal documents regulating their business relationships or interests. Imagine several shareholders who lack official documents pertaining to the distribution of shares and profits.

At the end of the first fiscal period, one of the shareholders says, "I deserve 60 percent of the profits because I have put many more hours into this business than any of you."

Another says, "No, I'm the one who deserves 60 percent because I invested the most capital to create this business."

And a third says, "No, I deserve 60 percent because I was the one who got the customers." Misunderstandings like these have ruined great friendships and businesses.

In the same way, a marriage contract should clearly define the clauses that protect the parties involved, especially the most vulnerable, such as children. There are many cases in family court consisting of emotionally wounded men and women, abandoned children, and parents who are trying to avoid their most basic and primitive responsibility: taking care of their offspring.

A Contract Contains Clear Clauses

During a live interview on national television, a lady called asking what to do with her "life's most important investment and endeavor," since there have been red flags in her relationship for the past four years. At the moment I thought, Oh no, here is one of those tricky questions. However, I tried to focus on her real need and struggle. Immediately something came to my mind. I told her, "Did you know that most of the businesses we know and regard as great success stories were once at the brink of closing their doors? However, they decided not to close their doors; to keep trying, to keep fighting, and to make it work. Besides, there is nothing that brings more meaning and satisfaction to the human spirit than having an adverse and losing situation and transforming it into a victory.

Most of us have had the opportunity to witness a wedding. It is a unique and beautiful ceremony. Full of hopes and dreams, decorations, smiles on the faces of young and old, upbeat music, abundant food, and tears of joy from the parents of the couple. All the attention is on the bride and groom; they unite us in the joy of the occasion. However, if we're not careful, the beauty of the sacred ceremony can distract us from the solemn words spoken by the minister, who publicly specifies the clauses of the marriage contract. When the minister asks the bride and groom, "Do you take this man/woman to be your lawfully wedded husband/wife, forgetting all others? Do you promise to love, honor, and respect him/her, in wealth or poverty, in health or sickness, till death do you part?" He or she is giving the couple the guidelines for their new contractual relationship; they set the three *"Clauses of the Marriage Contract of Marriage, Serious Business."*

The Exclusivity Clause

An *exclusivity clause* is a common practice in the business world. It is implemented in order to insure that the employee's mind, time and resources will be completely focused and dedicated to the company's mission.

Likewise, marriage requires an exclusivity clause. As a matter of fact, the term husband and wife is a unique title, accorded to the couple that has chosen to share an exclusive relationship with each other. These titles are governed by a contract before God and the laws of their country. This kind of exclusivity allows for the development of "two of the *Main Key Ingredients of Marriage, Serious Business*" in any successful marriage: *trust* and *intimacy*. When this exclusivity is broken, the trust in our marriage is damaged and as a result, intimacy is destroyed.

Exclusivity goes beyond faithfulness. It implies that an employee will be present and fully involved in the company. One of the most frequent complaints that wives have is that their spouses are not there for them. As you can see, many husbands are being faithful but not necessarily exclusive!

The Perseverance Clause

The second question, "Do you promise to love, honor, and respect him/her in wealth or poverty, in health or sickness…?" establishes what is called the *perseverance clause*. Marriage is a contract to stay together, accompany each other, and persevere under any and all circumstances. In other words, we are promising God and society that we will be with this person in good times and bad times, for better or worse, as much when everything goes wrong as when all goes well. As you can see, this kind of commitment has little to do with emotions and feelings. It is a commitment to persevere and to move forward no matter what or whom gets on the way. It is not just when you feel a passionate love for him or her, or "butterflies in your stomach." It is not a love born solely out of romance or attraction, but of the will and determination to fulfill what we promised the day we made the commitment at the altar, it is very serious business!

The Durability Clause

The last part of the minister's statement sets the foundation for the *durability clause*. It is not like that popular joke "Until 'Deb' do us part." Death is the only cause for termination in this contractual relationship. So what's the hurry to get married? Marriage is very serious business, the most important investment and endeavor in life. It's the cornerstone of any society, the incubator that ensures the emotional and spiritual welfare of our children, and the partnership that brings the most significant benefits and leaves behind the best legacy to this world and society: good men and women of character who display the *"5 Great Codes of Life of Marriage, Serious Business."* The best benefits are harvested in the years to come, do not give up, and set your mind to embark in a lifelong endeavor.

Conclusion

Even though Amanda and Jake are progressive and modern people, this does not ensure that their views about marriage benefits the couple the most. The fact that something is trendy or fashionable doesn't mean it's better or more beneficial. According to Robert H. Coombs, married people live longer and are usually physically and emotionally healthier than those who are not married.[14] Those who cohabit before marriage have a divorce rate of 50 percent to 100 percent higher than those who have not cohabited.[15] People who engage in premarital sex with someone other than their spouse "quite often" tend to be unfaithful in their marriages.[16] There is a much higher rate of domestic violence among those who cohabit than among those who are married.[17] Women cohabiting reported much higher rates of depression than women in a marriage relationship, followed only by those who have divorced a second time.[18]

As we can see, Amanda and Jake's modern view of cohabiting is not supported by scientific research. Marriage is still the most effective model and brings better results in all areas measured. The business world could help us again have a clearer picture. Stuart is seeking to invest capital in one of two companies and option A provides him with a lower rate of profitability and a higher risk even though it is the option that everybody is talking about, would it be very difficult for Stuart to choose option B? When it comes to investing wisely, do we base where we put our money on popular opinion, or figures that reflect performance?

How much more should marriage, the most important investment and endeavor in life, be carefully planned and wisely chosen? We should not be surprised that so many marriages are failing. Not because the model of marriage does not work, but due to this distorted image of marriage that has prevailed in pop culture; one that eclipses the importance of regarding marriage as very serious business, as life's most important investment and endeavor.

In restructuring our partnerships, we have to dig deeper to look at what marriage really implies and why it should be protected and regulated by a legal agreement between the parties. In doing this, husbands and wives are ready to join together as a one-of-a-kind partnership to embark on a lifelong project. One that is very serious business and can provide great benefits for them and a remarkable legacy for their children. However, do you know what does it take to build a strong marriage partnership?

SOMETHING TO THINK ABOUT

Marriage is the one-of-a-kind contract that protects and regulates the loving relationship between a husband and a wife

Rule of the Game Two:

REGARD MARRIAGE AS AN ONGOING PARTNERSHIP

Objective

That each marriage partner understand that, as in any business enterprise, he or she should master a set of principles that requires time and an ongoing effort. This set of principles is called the Rules of the Game.

Partnership

- A contractual relationship between two or more persons carrying on a joint business venture that, because of its difficult nature, requires a joint effort where each partner brings to the table what they can do better, supplementing each partner's shortcomings.

Marriage Case Study

Roger and Meg have been married for five years. They have not realized how quickly time has passed or how they have grown apart. Meg is CEO of a transnational firm and was promoted to this senior management position very quickly. Even with the birth of Roger Jr., she has still managed to cope with her responsibilities. Roger is an entrepreneur and has been selected by a leading business magazine as Entrepreneur of the Year. Both have sought refuge in their jobs because they each feel that they cannot afford to fail.

Roger has made large investments of capital, labor, energy, and presence in his business. As a business administration graduate, he knows there are a number of principles and procedures that must be established if a business is to operate and function successfully in the long term. He believes that being present every day in the business, meeting customers and suppliers, and dealing with competition has made him a true entrepreneur.

However, for Roger and Meg, things at home are not going as well as they would like. When they married, they were very much in love, full of hopes and dreams, but now they find themselves on the brink of failure. Meg asks what would happen to their home if they both put in the same effort that they put into their work.

"Don't misunderstand me," says Meg. "I don't want to neglect our work, but I don't want to neglect our home either. For me, my husband and my son are the most important things in my life. However, what I do not understand is . . . what happened to us?"

"Yes," says Roger. "If our marriage were a business, I'd know what to do."

"That's right!" exclaims Meg. "What if we see our marriage as a serious business, as the most important investment and endeavor in our life?"

"You're right," says Roger with an enlightened expression. "Let's sit down and analyze how our marriage resembles a business and see how we can get ahead and succeed."

"Yes," Meg says enthusiastically. "After all, we are successful, and we will not allow our marriage to fail."

Main Topic

In the same way that Roger and Meg have never thought of marriage as their most important investment and endeavor in life, many couples go through life being successful in their business endeavors and careers, but feel incompetent when it comes to their own personal relationships. However, what would happen if, like Roger and Meg, we regard our marriage in such a way?

Marriage has many enemies. There are powerful entities in the world that want to tarnish the positive image of a family, an image that it has possessed for centuries. Recent studies show that one in two marriages end in divorce. This statistic has been exploited by some who claim that the traditional family model does not work, therefore, we must look for new alternatives. For years, the idea of a husband and a wife completely bored and frustrated in their marriage has been conveyed to us as the "true" image of marriage. The TV show Desperate Housewives became a success by portraying marriage as something boring and enslaving.

Knowing the Rules of the Game is an essential requirement for the success that we desire. Each of the rules presented in this book are foundational to the marriage partnership. The second Rule of the Game is to regard marriage as an ongoing partnership. What does it mean to regard marriage as a partnership? Marriage is, without doubt, an enterprise, a life project, and the most important investment in life. If everyone were to view marriage as such, it would be widely understood that certain requirements must be met before we can achieve the success we desire.

Choose your *Marriage Partner for Life*

The first requirement for building a successful business is choosing the right partner. This process is one of the most important decisions for the future success of any partnership. When one chooses a partner, possession of capital is not the only important factor. How many people have associated with someone who did possess the capital, but his or her worldview, values, and principles are so different from yours that they ended up bankrupting their partnership, and worse, friendship? Partnering with someone for the rest of our lives is a very serious decision. Even if one has not made the best possible choice, it is still possible to have a successful partnership. There is a set of principles and practices we call the Rules of the Game. If you learn, assimilate, internalize, implement, master and embody these rules, they will produce healthy and successful homes.

Define Your North

The second requirement is to define a "north," or a mission statement for the marriage partnership. A north, or desired end result, must include several objectives. The first objective is to understand that we are in this world to leave a legacy. We will cover that in Rule 10: Leave a legacy behind. The second objective is for our children to become good men and women. For that, we must instill in them the *5 Great Codes of Life* and the *5 Great Responsibilities of Parenting*, which we will discuss later. The third objective is that both husband and wife may achieve full development physically, emotionally, intellectually, and spiritually. The fourth goal is that we intentionally stay together, and plan each and every family activity with the clear motive of being together. The fifth goal is to develop an atmosphere in which understanding, self-control, acceptance, forgiveness, and high expectations prevail. The sixth goal is that we may discover the reason God put us together as a family, and placed us on this earth in this moment of history.

Steven L. McShane and Mary Ann Von Glinow corroborate this idea when they state, "Imagine an organization without goals. It would consist of a mass of people wandering around aimlessly without any sense of direction. Overall, as Vodafone's Grahame Maher stated, organizations consist of people with a collective sense of purpose. This purpose might not be fully understood or agreed upon, but it helps employees to engage in structured patterns of interaction. In other words, they expect each other to complete various tasks in a coordinated way—in an *organized* way."[19] Where could this idea be more important than in marriage? There has to be a clear understanding of where we are going, how we are going to get there, and an active engagement in the interactions that will take us there.

Invest

The third thing we must do is invest. We must invest our time, resources, knowledge, and heart into our marriage. All entrepreneurs know that if they are to see their endeavor thrive and emerge, they must give themselves wholeheartedly to their business. Likewise, in marriage we must invest ourselves in an enterprise that will bring the greatest dividends to our lives.

Look After Your Capital

The fourth requirement is to look after your capital. Not many employees will take care of the assets of the business as its owners would. If wealth is not cared for properly, the business will soon be bankrupt. In the same way, marriage contains capital made up not only of the material things, but also of its members and their dreams, goals, values, and life principles. This capital sustain and nourish the marriage partnership, and if properly safeguarded, can guarantee the desired success.

Follow a Set of Principles

The fifth requirement is to understand that there is a set of legal, financial, and marketing principles which govern a business, which are of universal application. Similarly, marriage has a set of principles that will produce the successes we are seeking in our marriages. These principles are what we call the Rules of the Game, and they should be known and mastered to achieve the desired result.

Value our Human Resources

The sixth requirement is to know that every business is composed of human beings, and proper interaction between the parties that comprise the business is essential to ensure its success. There is no reason to have the correct processes and an ideal product if the individuals involved cannot communicate and interact appropriately. If there is one place where mastering the art of interpersonal relationships is needed, it is at home. One can say that in this enterprise, life's most important investment and endeavor, harmony amongst its members is vital. This does not mean striving for perfection, but rather learning how to manage imperfection.

Grahame Maher, who leads Vodafone's operations in the Czech Republic, states, "A business is just a registered name of a piece of paper. It's nothing more than that unless there's a group of people who care about a common purpose for why they are, where they are going, how they are going to be when they are there."[20] It could not be truer for marriage. Partners need to have a common purpose and a clear understanding of their role in it.

Set your Functional Structure

The seventh requirement is to understand that every business must have a functional structure which allows it to carry out its mission and facilitate the product or service it wishes to provide. In a typical functional structure, there is usually a CEO, COO, and CFO; others might include marketing and sales managers, each of which have different functions. Although these people might all be capable and

Having this kind of information and knowledge can drastically change the way we value our relationships and marriages. However, the question is not whether we value our marriages, but how placing this value in our relationships can unleash a force that will fuel us in unimaginable and innovative ways. This is exactly what we are about to discuss next.

SOMETHING TO THINK ABOUT

The best and most profitable of all businesses is family.
Its profits and benefits not only reward their current
members but also transcend to future generations.

Rule of the Game Three:
HAVE VALUES AS
THE DRIVING FUEL

Objective

That each marriage partner will be able to understand how important values are and how they drive behavior in a marriage partnership.

Values

- The fuel that drives a person to live boldly for something.
- The resources that drive a business to keep the doors open.

Marriage Case Study

Tony and Valerie have been married for two years. Tony comes from a home characterized by divorce; all the marriages of his aunts and uncles have ended in divorce, but Tony considers himself different. He greatly values his marriage and cannot conceive in his mind the possibility that one day his own marriage may come to an end. Many of his relatives, discussing their marital failures, were convinced that their partners were totally incompatible with them. Even those personally embittered were able to identify the "huge" differences between themselves and their partners, which they claimed were primarily responsible for the failures in their marriages.

"My former wife and I were very different," said Uncle Carson. "She liked to watch TV and I did not." This "huge" difference is the blame for Uncle Carson's marital failure, according to him.

If we had the opportunity to hear from all of Tony's aunts and uncles, we would realize that their marriages were ended by trifles rather than serious and sensitive matters.

On the other hand, Valerie comes from a family in which there has never been a single divorce. Before she married, her father told her, "Honey, marriage is not easy. Indeed, it is very difficult. There are many excuses we could use to talk us out of expending the effort required to continually and successfully pursue this great endeavor. However, we place a higher value on having a successful marriage than we do the excuses that prevent us from making the investment required to maintain it successfully. It's a great institution that brings value and benefits to its members and the community."

He paused, looking into her eyes and holding her hand. "Honey, every time you want to run away from your marriage, focus on the things that united you in the beginning, not the pressing things that may try to divide you. And never forget how many people would end up wounded and affected if this wonderful partnership you are starting failed." No doubt, Tony's family does value marriage in the way they profess, but Valerie's family considers marriage really important.

Main Topic

Like Tony and Valerie, many engage in marriage without even thinking of what value they place on it. The fact that I am in love with someone and decided to spend the rest of my life with that person doesn't mean that I value marriage as a model, as the vehicle that can take me to the destination where I want to arrive. Most people ignore how powerful values are in their lives. They are the driving force and fuel that moves them every day to get out of their beds and do what they value.

Values can be defined as the set of perspectives, beliefs, norms, expectations, and behaviors that express one's philosophy of life and govern the interactions of this person with his or her environment. In other words, values are the fuel that move or drive a person to think and act in a certain way. Values are those things that determine what we do with our lives.

Those who study organizational behavior are familiar with several popular books about the topic. Values are the new motto and the foundation for many business transformations in recent years. "Values represent the unseen magnet that pulls employees in the same direction."[23]

In this book we present a series of rules that constitute the foundation of the marriage partnership. The third Rule of the Game is to have values as the driving fuel. What do you think is meant by values as the driving fuel? The following model of how our values interact with our perceptions, attitudes, emotions, and behavior attempts to explain how and why we act and feel one way or another. It is not a tiered model. The interaction occurs from the top down, bottom up, and sideways. We present it in stages to simplify our explanation.

Vital Values versus Trivial Values

There are two types of values: vital and trivial, what we have identify as "*Vital and Trivial Values of Marriage, Serious Business.*" Vital values are those that we stick to, no matter what. They do not depend on the environment but on an extraordinary and unstoppable inner strength that makes us do what we strongly believe to be most important. We could say they're our convictions. For example, a vital value for Margaret is punctuality. Whatever happens, she always arrives fifteen minutes early for all of her commitments. Being on time is a strong conviction that governs her behavior.

On the other hand, trivial values are those that we say are important to us, but excuses can often override them. For example, Robert and Charlie consider it very important to exercise. They have set out to run at five o'clock in the morning every day. Beep, beep, beep, beep! The alarm went off. As soon as Robert heard the lousy sound, he reached out to snooze it. He wanted to continue sleeping but remembered the commitment he made with Charlie. He stretched out, and making a great effort sat up at the edge of his bed. He looked out the window and noticed that the window was foggy. He immediately reacted and said, "I'm not going because it's very cold," and after a pause, he added, "I will go tomorrow. Yes, that's what I will do."

That night before going to bed, he set the alarm again. He was so tired, he didn't even realize when he went to sleep. Beep, beep, beep, beep! The alarm went off just as the day before. As soon as he heard the lousy sound, he reached out to snooze it. As usual, he wanted to continue sleeping but remembered the commitment he made with Charlie. "I don't want to let him down again today," he whispered. He stretched out, and making a great effort sat up at the edge of his bed. He looked through the window and noticed that it was raining. He immediately reacted and said, "I am not getting wet," and after a pause, he added, "I will go tomorrow. Yes, that's what I will do."

That night as in the past two nights, he set the alarm again. All of the sudden, the alarm went off "Beep, beep, beep!" As soon as he heard the lousy sound, he grabbed his cell phone to check the time and said, "How can this be, it's already time? I can't get up. I didn't sleep well." Turning around and pulling the covers over his face, he went back to sleep. Exercising is really a trivial value for Robert. Be that as it may, Robert always has an excuse for not getting up.

Charlie, on the other hand, is ready to go every morning at five o'clock, whether it rains, thunders, snows, or he had a bad night. As you can tell, for Charlie, exercising is indeed a vital value. This kind of determination is unconscious and habitual, since it has been obtained throughout life. Our pasts, what and who influenced us as kids and how that impacted and marked us, determine our present identity. Our perceptions of life's tangibles and intangibles are filtered and determined by what is important to us, our values. It is important to emphasize that even though we acquire most of our values early in life, they can be modified or altered by strong experiences or by a slow process of awareness that leads us to new ones. If we really want to know what our values are, we just need to take a look at what we are dedicating our time and effort to and how we invest our money and resources. Examining ourselves in this way can be very frustrating, yet revealing. It is never too late, however; as even adults can modify their values and acquire new ones.

If we really want to succeed in our marriage partnerships, it is essential that we make our marriages and families vital values. Values are the foundation for everything in life. A little over two thousand years ago, Jesus of Nazareth said, "Where your treasure is, there your heart will be also."[24] Jesus asserted that what we consider important and of value in our lives determines where our hearts are.

Our Values Determine Our Perceptions

Once while we were waiting in the emergency room of a hospital near our house, a mother with two children came through the doors where patients were being attended to and took their seats in the waiting room, or, rather, the mother took a seat while her children explored the area with reckless abandon. The two little troublemakers were passing under and over every single chair across the aisles, regardless of whether they were occupied by an adult in pain. We felt discomfort and anger because we value discipline, order, and manners. These values determined the filters or perceptions that we use to see what was happening around us.

While those unrestrained little rascals were about to drive us all crazy, our values made us perceive their behavior in that situation as impermissible. Why? Because when we value something, we filter everything through what we value. What was happening in that emergency room did not conform to our values of discipline, order, and manners, and, consequently, we regarded the two children's behavior as antagonistic and even offensive. We use our values to filter everything that comes through our senses. This allows us to understand why people see things so differently and in so many different ways.

Our Perceptions Determine Our Attitudes

Our perceptions determine the attitudes that we assume towards life, people, and possessions. Normally these attitudes are generated unconsciously; therefore, we do not always notice them. Nevertheless, they determine how other people perceive us. Not surprisingly, many times the way other people treat us is a reflection of the attitudes we have projected onto them. The same happens in marriage. Many times the way a couple reacts to a situation reflects the attitudes that they have been projecting onto each other. For instance, if I am rude to my wife, it should not surprise me when she becomes defensive or defiant in return.

That day in the emergency room we realized that the perceptions we formed about that mother and her children were the result of our values. That is, our desire for discipline, order, and manners rendered that situation intolerable and generated unfavorable attitudes in our hearts toward the mother, such as rejection, intolerance, and apathy.

The Designer of marriage wants us to work on the attitudes we display at home. Therefore we must first determine what kind of values we have concerning marriage and how those values shape our perceptions of our marriage partnership. These perceptions, in turn, shape our attitudes toward our marriage partnership. Sometimes these perceptions lead us to negative attitudes. For example, a wife who perceives that her husband does not place the same value on marriage, her vital value, can develop negative attitudes toward him, such as disrespect, and lead her to seek opportunities to undermine him.

Given that marriage constitutes the most important investment and endeavor in life, how can I be aware of the attitudes that I'm having toward my marriage partner? Most of us can be aware of the kind of attitudes we are displaying at home. However, if we have problems figuring them out, all we have to do is ask our relatives, coworkers, or friends, and they will make sure to point them out to us right away.

Our Attitudes Determine Our Emotions

Our attitudes have a surprising effect on our emotions. That day in the emergency room we experienced a series of negative emotions. It was outrageous. Watching that mother fail her children infuriated us. However, there was something that changed our feelings dramatically toward this woman. A nurse came out of the emergency room and said, "Your husband is out of danger; he has been moved to intensive care." Apparently he survived a heart attack. When we heard that, everything changed. Why? Because we also value human life, mercy, and compassion, and these values helped us perceive the woman in a different light, changing our attitudes towards her and, as a result, our emotions as well.

Current research in[25] neuroscience indicates that the information apprehended by our five senses is channeled both to our cognitive and our emotional centers. This is a new discovery, as previous research did not take into account the emotions as key factors in our mental processes. Apparently, when information enters our brains, the emotional center determines whether that information threatens the things that drive or move us to act by assigning it what are called "emotional markers." These assigned emotional markers are not coldly calculated sensations but spontaneous and innate. Thus, although we try to logically assess a situation, our brains have already assigned emotional markers to it, influencing our cognitive process one way or another.

Our Emotions Determine Our Behavior

It is extremely important that we understand that changes in our values result in changes in our perceptions, which, in turn, result in changes in perceptions, attitudes, emotions, and, ultimately, behaviors. Usually, the way a boyfriend treats his girlfriend is not the same way he treats other people. Why? Because the way he treats her stems from the value he gives her. The value he assigns her cultivates his favorable perception of her, generating attitudes of appreciation, admiration, tolerance, and dedication, which produce positive emotions capable of changing his behavior towards her. If for some reason the value he has for her changes, how he perceives her will vary, his attitudes towards her will start changing, and his behavior towards her will reflect those new attitudes.

All marriages go through difficult times. In some situations we manifest negative attitudes that can lead us to criticize our marriage partners or treat them with indifference. Or we may end up undermining each other. When our marriage partners express these attitudes, we can become angry, lose respect, and feel disappointed and disillusioned. It is therefore essential that we work on changing our behaviors, especially if we realize that our attitudes are compromising our marriages by devaluing how we perceive our partner. We must change our attitudes, and in changing our attitudes, we must assimilate new perceptions and ways of seeing our marriage partnership and our marriage partner. To achieve this, we must be clear about what are and should be our values. What value must we give our partner and the marriage partnership we decided to undertake together?

We change our attitudes and learn how to react to criticism, indifference, contempt, and anger by understanding that there is a greater purpose, something that is a lot more valuable and important to us as individual partners. In other words, the "business" as a whole is more important than the individual partners who comprise it. If the business succeeds, the partners succeed; if the business loses, the partners will also lose. As the saying goes, "We must know which battles to fight." We choose such battles by having a greater purpose in mind.

That greater purpose is choosing to regard marriage as very serious business. It's the value we place on staying together, on creating the kind of atmosphere, unity, and strength that will allow the partnership to grow, succeed, and find the refuge we all need in the midst of this wild jungle. It is also to wish for our children better lives and futures. That is the type of fuel that drives the kind of home we all want. The fundamental reason we share a family is to leave a positive footprint on those around us, starting with our children and not stopping until we reach the entire world.

Conclusion

We've all heard about the importance of values in life. We talk about how many believe that people have lost their values and how others appear to lack values. The reality is there is no such thing as an absence of values. What actually happens is that the person who appears to lack values simply possesses a different or opposed set of them. For example, a person who does not mind stepping over other people to get richer is a person whose vital value is to become rich at any price.

Just as we saw in the case of Tony and Valerie, people can come from homes that assign different values to family and marriage. How many of us have been advised to value marriage as Valerie's father counseled her? What values have we inherited from our parents about marriage? As we can see, like Tony and his family, many people do not give marriage the appropriate value it needs to have in order to succeed.

Values determine our perceptions. Our perceptions shape our attitudes, our attitudes ignite our emotions, and our emotions influence our actions. The same is true in marriage; each partner has a unique set of values. Sometimes these values may conflict with what is necessary for the proper functioning and success of marriage. For example, if a man's close friends are more important to him than his wife, his lack of value for marriage will obviously result in attitudes that may adversely affect his relationship with his wife. Such attitudes will eventually manifest as harmful and detrimental actions every time that man prefers going out with his friends to taking care of his wife and family.

These values are the fuel that drives people in one of two directions. One leads to the path of happiness and family fulfillment, and the other leads to unhappiness and disruption of our marriage partnerships. Therefore it is imperative that we make a vital value of our marriages. These values can also affect our relationships with loved ones and third parties, leading to unhealthy dependencies in those relationships. In the following chapter, we will address the need to cut the "umbilical cord" of any dependency that threatens the stability and success of life's most important investment and endeavor, marriage.

SOMETHING TO THINK ABOUT
Values are the fuel that drives our lives.

Rule of the Game Four:
CUT THE UMBILICAL CORD

Objective

That each marriage partner might be able to understand the importance of starting and maintaining a marriage partnership free from the interference of third parties.

Umbilical Cord

- Set of vessels linking the mother's placenta with her baby's belly so that the baby is nourished until birth.
- Used to describe someone who has an unhealthy dependency on others.

Marriage Case Study

Jeff and Samantha are going through a difficult time in their marriage. Both have developed a certain degree of resentment. However, their guilt neutralizes them and makes them believe that the other is reacting badly in the wrong.

Jeff complains that Samantha relies excessively on her mother, saying, "We cannot have the slightest discussion because she runs and hides behind her mom. Not only that, but she pulls money from our budget to help her siblings and parents without asking me anything."

"Jeff rarely includes me in any decision pertaining to what we are doing," Samantha says. "Every Sunday we have to go to his parents' home—no other plan is an option. Besides, he always tells me that his mother comes first, before anybody, including me. How can he complain about me running to my mother when he tells me all the time that there is no one more important to him than his mother?"

Samantha frequently complains that her mother-in-law is always interfering in everything she does at home. "She is constantly telling me that Jeff is used to seeing things done for him this way or that Jeff doesn't like it when someone cooks for him this or that. And if this is not enough, when my mother-in-law makes a comment about how something should be done at home, Jeff talks down to me as if to say, "'What are you waiting for? Just do it the way my mom is telling you.'"

The resentment between Jeff and Samantha is growing.

"What can we do?" Samantha sighs, "Is there hope for us?"

Main Topic

If there is an issue that affects most couples today, it is that of third-party involvement. Just like Jeff and Samantha, many ignore how devastating and detrimental this can be.

There is an old adage that says, "Before you marry, be sure of a house wherein to tarry." However, we most often think of that wise saying only in terms of a physical place to live. When we are at the altar, the minister—regardless of our religious affiliation—uses a marital formula that specifies the *clauses* of this new contractual relationship. He can put it in different ways, but at some point he tells us that "a man shall leave his father and mother." This phrase is the basis for the fourth Rule of the Game: cut the umbilical cord. What does cutting the umbilical cord imply?

Julie and Richard agreed to start a new business. Both had relatives and business savvy friends who gave them countless ideas and suggestions for how to conduct their business. Based on the talents, skills, and backgrounds of each partner, they chose the kind of business they wanted to start and how they would manage it. What do you think would happen to this business if Richard decided to run to his family and friends to ask what he needed to do every time he has a disagreement with Julie? Do his family and friends have a say in what decision should be made in this business?

What would happen to their business if Richard placed more importance on what his family and friends have to say about how to manage the business than what his partner, Julie, thinks? Where do you think the business would end up if any of the partners placed the recommendations of others over the wishes and decisions of his/her partner? This would be something unheard of in the business world! It is important that we clarify that the problem does not reside in rejecting, ignoring, or despising what our partner advises us, but in giving more importance and weight to our friends and family's opinions and desires than our partner's.

Unhealthy Dependency on Your Parents

The first thing we can deduce from this rule is that from the moment we decide to start our marriage partnership, priorities must change. As children we were under the protection and companionship of our parents; our first priority and object of loyalty was the home to which we belonged as sons and daughters. Now our priority must be the new marriage partnership we are building. Our marriage is not a branch of our parents' marriage but a new and autonomous partnership. According to the Designer, our first and foremost priority in this new partnership must be our new partner. Our second priority should be our children; lastly, our final priority should be our parents. Only this model will allow for the healthy development of a new family without the unduly influence of third parties—a family without divided loyalties.

This is what it really means to leave our parents. This "leaving" is not about neglecting the emotional or economical support of our parents; nor is it the end of having a healthy, effective relationship with them. Rather, it is to stop depending on them at least in three respects. First, we have to cut the umbilical cord financially. Marriage partners need to get ahead financially on their own. This builds the necessary responsibility required to make a marriage partnership work. It also develops the respect and admiration needed to maintain such an undertaking, which fuels husbands' basic needs. It does not mean that parents cannot lend their kids a helping hand in difficult times. But it does mean that children should not expect their parents to pull them out of every difficulty they may get into.

Second, cut your umbilical cord emotionally. Marriage partners must cut off unhealthy emotional dependence on their parents. That is, they have to take responsibility for solving their own emotional conflicts. Despite the fact that there has been an eternal emotional connection between parent and child since childhood, they should assume responsibility for addressing differences and disappointments in their marriages themselves. Nonetheless, there are still husbands and wives who, at the first sign of problems with their spouses, run back to their parents and hide under their wings.

Third, cut your umbilical cord spiritually. Both spouses must stop depending spiritually on their parents. They are no longer under the spiritual guidance of their parents. Now it's time for husbands to take responsibility and start a whole new adventure of spiritual leadership, both for themselves and for their wives and children. This requires investing time in their beliefs in order to strengthen their relationships with God. It may require a reevaluation of their religious traditions to determine why they do what they do; perhaps even a decision between religious traditions or a spiritual relationship with God.

Unhealthy Dependency from Your Parents

Parents should allow their children to develop and mature. When a father or mother always runs to the aid of their children, they turn them into "parasites," adults that will never be capable of assuming responsibility. Even when mothers or fathers have the best intentions, this type of interference in the marriage partnership of their children will only bring countless problems, undermine the foundations of the marriage partnership, and may eventually destroy it. The best wedding gift fathers and mothers can give to their sons or daughters is allowing them to develop an autonomous marriage partnership, free of any unhealthy interference.

Unhealthy Relationships with Your Friends

One of the most serious problems faced by many marriages today is the intervention of friends in their marriage partnership. When many people get married, they do not want the slightest change in their relationships with their buddies or gals. In fact, they may tell their friends that nothing will change and everything will continue to be exactly the same. This mind-set is as absurd as leaving one company to work for a competitor while telling the co-workers from the former company that nothing will change in their working relationship, that everything will remain the same.

Again, it is not about putting aside your friends but reorganizing your new priorities. Now your duty and care should be the new marriage partnership you have started. Your friends must understand that you cannot make decisions in isolation anymore without taking into account the insight or opinion of your marriage partner. You must tell your friends to stop any attempt at third-party interference in the internal affairs of your marriage partnership. Can you imagine one business interfering in the internal affairs of another, telling management how things should be done? Why should we think that in the most important business of all, our marriage partnership, it would work well?

In regards to you and your partner, if you do not cut out the interference of others—and remember that you have an exclusivity clause—you will fail to establish a real sense of teamwork in your partnership. This will consequently lower the chances of developing a true relationship of mutual trust and loyalty, ending any realistic possibility of success and personal fulfillment. In marriage, you cannot have success and satisfaction in the absence of this rule at home because it will become a marriage in which third parties frequently interfere. They may have the best intentions, but they will ultimately harm the welfare of the most important investment and endeavor in your life.

Most people who enter a marriage partnership are unaware of the tragic consequences that come with the influence of others, especially when that influence comes from people we appreciate and love. We should not confuse one thing with another; cutting the umbilical cord does not mean withdrawing value or affection from our loved ones. To cut the umbilical cord is to recognize the harmful effects that can manifest through the unhealthy influence and interference of others in a marriage partnership. It is important to acknowledge and accept that to achieve success and fulfillment, we must solve things as a couple, giving priority to our husbands or wives. By doing this, we will build a relationship of true intimacy, respect, trust, esteem, and loyalty. These *Marriage Partnership Main Key ingredients* increase the chances of success and family welfare and give us the opportunity to make the road ahead less difficult.

Conclusion

Like Jeff and Samantha, many couples are not fully aware of the level of unhealthy emotional dependence they have toward their parents or friends. Nor do they see clearly and impartially the degree of interference that can infiltrate their marriages. The ironic thing is that they can easily detect the unhealthy dependence and interference in their partners' parents and friends. That is why there are so many jokes about mother-in-laws and "momma's boys" or "daddy's girls." It's like this popular saying, "There is no one as blind as the one who refuses to see." Recognizing the importance of establishing this Rule of the Game, as we have explained above, is the first step towards a successful marriage partnership. This step encourages the development of an autonomous enterprise that allows all parties to fully develop while experiencing full and satisfying relationships with parents, relatives, and friends.

It is the responsibility of every marriage partner to talk affectionately and tactfully with their parents or friends about the importance of cutting the umbilical cord, whether they are interfering, and whether partners in the partnership are still dependent on them in unhealthy ways. Tact and love do not take away firmness and courage. This Rule of the Game clears the path and paves the road to intentionally becoming a one-of-a-kind team, one that will endure the strongest winds blowing against their lives' most important investment and endeavor. The question is, how can you and your marriage partner become such a team? That's exactly what we are about to see in the following chapter.

SOMETHING TO THINK ABOUT
By cutting the umbilical cord, we unleash
a healthy and autonomous marriage partnership.

Rule of the Game Five:

GLUE TOGETHER AS ONE

Objective

That each marriage partner will understand the concept of *"Glue Together as One"* in the marriage partnership and how this concept may transform the state of the marriage partnership forever

Glue Together as One

- The idea of two becoming one; together as one.
- The quality or state of being a complete and indivisible team.

Marriage Case Study

Martin and Mary crossed the threshold of marriage with many dreams and expectations. It had been almost a year when their first difficulties surfaced. Mary began to feel some resentment toward Martin. This feeling grew as the days passed. Far from improving, the anxiety of finding a solution grew virtually unmanageable. Finally, Mary decided to sit down with Martin and discuss the matter. She began by saying that she was tired of his late arrivals, especially when she had to stay at home alone with the dinner ready. She said she deeply resented the fact that he was late without communicating anything to her. Martin did not appreciate her observation. He was offended.

"I don't think I should have to give an explanation of where I am. I did not get married to be treated like a child," he said.

Martin grew up in a household where his father was a doctor and his mother was a nurse. Both had conflicting schedules. The family ate at odd times and had become accustomed to coming and going freely without having to give any explanation. Mary, on the other hand, grew up in a household where both parents were employed by the government, leaving for work at the same time in the morning and always arriving back home at four o'clock in the afternoon. They ate at six o'clock and had family time around the table during dinner.

Main Topic

As we can see, Martin and Mary came from homes with different customs, and because of those differences, are facing an adverse situation in their own home. Mary was frustrated that her previous customs and family values did not coincide with those of Martin, who, in his opinion, was not doing anything wrong.

Induction Process

Any person who enters a marriage must recognize the potential need to conform to a new situation. It's like leaving one job for another. It is likely that you may not succeed in the new job by trying to do things the way you did in the former company. Doing so may only damage your chances of acceptance and promotion in the new company.

Likewise, our marriage partnership is an institution in itself, requiring us to conform to its own conditions, rules, and culture. Successful companies obtain a system in which new employees go through called an induction process. Through this process the employees become acquainted with the values, rituals, and culture of the organization. Husbands and wives must go through an induction process as well, which helps shape them as a new marriage partnership, making it a matter of serious business. That's why we recommend that couples wait a couple of years before having children in order to facilitate this process. This also coincides with that period in life where we develop our adult habits.

In this book we have been presenting a series of rules that are the cornerstones of a marriage partnership. The fifth Rule of the Game is Glue Together as One. What do we mean by glue together as one? What does the minister mean when he says, "The two shall become one flesh?"

The phrase "glue together as one" implies two concepts—unity and diversity. The idea is that we can achieve indivisible unity while preserving our diversity and our sense of being unique.

Glued Together

There was a form of glue advertised on TV a few years back that came in a pack with two pieces of dough of different colors wrapped separately. To make this glue work, both halves must be softened and then mixed together until both colors become one single color. Applying this to our marriage partnership, we must be willing to let go and sacrifice the things that we cling relentlessly to because these things compromise unity. As already mentioned, to achieve that effect in the glue, we must begin to soften the halves that are hardened; then one can be mixed with the other so that these two different masses fulfill their purpose together. These two masses were designed to work together, not separately.

This is what we mean by glue together as one in our marriage partnership. It implies that each spouse complements the other; that to be truly effective in our marriage we should soften and shape ourselves for the other, even when we have different preferences and backgrounds. We must be willing to amalgamate to form a new marriage partnership. This process of "mixing" may mean the loss of things from our pasts, but now there is a new home with its own characteristics. We must, through the mixing process, establish an intimate union so deep that we glue spiritually and functionally together as one.

There are some phrases that signal the absence of this rule. Phrases such as "My mom used to" or "We used to do it this way" or "We never used to do so" are the kind of statements that break this rule. Couples must diligently be aware of their habits and resist all barriers that oppose this rule if they want to experience the great benefits of gluing together as one in purpose, values, and worldview. However, in this process there always tends to be a stronger partner. In these cases, most of the time the strong partner imposes his or her desires, customs, and beliefs on the weak partner who, by trying to avoid conflict or discussions, puts aside his or her ways. This kind of vicious behavioral cycle does not produce a healthy and successful relationship in any couple. On the contrary, the weak person is silenced and starts accumulating resentment, often to the point of explosion or implosion. When that occurs, it is too late for the marriage partnership. Remember, what makes a business successful is not the selfish desires of its partners, demanding one thing or another. It is the ability to do what's best for the business. If the business succeeds, the partners succeed; if the business fails, the partners fail.

Conflicting Agendas

Couples will be unable to truly have a sense of intimacy and teamwork in the absence of this rule in their homes because it will be a marriage in which each member has his or her own agenda. Just as a business cannot thrive well without a sense of teamwork, unity, and purpose, the marriage partnership cannot succeed without this sense of gluing together as one. Can you conceive of a business where employees come to do their jobs and perform the tasks and duties as they please or did in their previous workplaces? What kind of business could survive like that? What kind of products or services could be generated in the midst of such chaos? Every business requires a sense of togetherness if it seeks to achieve its goals in an efficient and effective way.

Conclusion

It is critical for couples to understand as early as possible in their marriage that intentionally gluing together as one is an important part of the Rules of the Game, one that helps them drive their marriage partnerships to success and avoid a lot of headaches and unnecessary conflicts. Like Martin and Mary, many couples enter the threshold of marriage without being aware or having a clear understanding of how their different backgrounds can affect the stability of their marriage partnership. This lack of understanding may cause conditions in their relationships to worsen if the couples do not know or ignore the induction process of glue together as one.

Martin did not understand why he should be accountable to his wife. Growing up, he never had to tell anyone where he was or at what time he was coming and going. According to his parents' values, that was the way to establish a relationship of maturity, confidence, and independence. But Mary did not perceive it that way. For her it represented the very opposite: a sign of neglect and disinterest.

As you can see, the fact that marriage partners come from different backgrounds is not only a matter of the past, but it also affects their perceptions; and perceptions affect how they feel and the attitudes that they assume. Perceptions affect their actions and decisions. Just think of the possible decisions that Martin and Mary can make at this point in their marriage life. If they allow themselves to be carried away by their perceptions and the heat of the moment, it is more likely they will head in a direction that leads their marriage partnership to failure. Once the couple understands this, commits to softening and mixing, and intentionally gluing together as one, they will be on a path to a new marriage partnership, one characterized by a unity of thought and purpose that reflects the fact that they have "become one flesh."

Each marriage is unique in nature and should not attempt to copy others. But each marriage must apply the principles and Rules of the Game to be healthy and achieve the desired goal, to be glued together as one. If Martin and Mary do not become aware that the diverse elements in their backgrounds can seriously affect their marriage, they will not recognize the need to soften and mix together, forming a new dynamic that allows them to rediscover and redefine themselves. If we, in the same way, ignore the potential seriousness of our differences and backgrounds, and we believe that by ignoring them, they will disappear, then we are very wrong. There cannot be a true softening and mixing without giving, sacrificing, and changing our customs, habits, and old perceptions. This kind of commitment represents one of the phases in the *"Pyramid of True Love of Marriage, Serious Business."* One of the most beautiful adventures of marriage is undertaking our journey through the river of diversity, like paddling in a two-seated canoe, working as a team that has been glued together as one. Only then can we navigate through the rapids of life without sinking.

However, in order to do that we must understand first what our roles are and how we can lead this extraordinary endeavor to success.

SOMETHING TO THINK ABOUT
Each marriage partner must soften, mix, and glue together
as one to build a new and unique marriage partnership.

Rule of the Game Six:
EXERCISE FRONTLINE LEADERSHIP

Objective
That husbands, as part of a managerial team, understand the importance of exercising the unique and specific frontline leadership role that they have in their "marriage partnership," and how that role could impact and redefine their marriage partnership.

Marriage Partnership Frontline Leadership
- The action of being the head, the CEO of life's most important investment and endeavor.
- To step up and take the lead.
- Lead by example.

Marriage Case Study

Carol does not like the idea of buying a house that is closer to her husband's new workplace. She does not want to leave the neighborhood since that would mean moving away from her mother.

"I do not understand why Chris wants to move there. I've spent my entire life in this neighborhood. My mom and family live really close, and I don't want to move away. It seems very selfish of Chris to ask me to leave my family," says Carol. "Besides, it is also a safer area for our children, John, Mike, and Joe, to grow up in."

Chris has been working for fourteen years at the same company, and he just got a promotion in another part of town that allows him to double his salary and spend more time with his family.

"I have been waiting for this opportunity for years," says Chris. "This will give me the time I need to spend with my wife and children while earning twice what I earn now. I do not understand how Carol can be so blind. I understand why she is so attached to her mother, but at the end of the day our children and I are her family now."

In addition, John and Mike do not want to leave their friends.

"All my friends are here. Now dad is asking us to leave behind what is most important to us. If he wants to move, let him move alone," says Mike with frustration, supported by a nod from John.

Chris also wants to move their children from the neighborhood because of drugs, particularly cocaine, among the more affluent students in their school district. However, knowing the issues, Carol and her children decide to vote on the matter and communicate their decision to Chris, "We are not leaving."

Main Topic

Just like Carol and Chris, hundreds and hundreds of couples enter marriage without really knowing the functions and roles each should play in their new partnership. Many think that marriage is just a stunning wedding ceremony with an expensive reception. Others see it as the pursuit of happiness and romance. Even those who have a clearer concept of what marriage is about, do not fully understand the roles that each partner should be fulfilling.

There is a series of rules that constitute the cornerstones of every marriage partnership. The sixth Rule of the Game is to exercise frontline leadership. What does exercising frontline leadership imply? What is the role husbands should play as part of the leadership team that we have denominated "*Managerial Team of Marriage, Serious Business?*"

When it comes to a business, the CEO is part of a managerial team that unites to carry on the desires of the board and executing the actions necessary to carry out those goals by showing strong frontline leadership. This type of leadership entails a clear vision of where they are heading, a sense of pride and belonging among employees, and a high profit for the owners and significant benefits for the employees. Frontline leadership is essential to carry out the mission and vision of the business. It is also important for safeguarding the company's assets and capital, gaining market positioning, empowering and rewarding employees' performance, and celebrating business achievements.

When it comes to the marriage partnership, the managerial team is made up of both husband and wife, each with very specific roles to play in this managerial team. These roles, like in any other business, have to be performed and carried out by the person assigned to each position, whether the CEO, CFO, COO, etc. The role does not define the capacity, value, or contribution to the bottom line of each leader in the managerial team. However, they were appointed to those positions because of the skills, leadership, experience, and knowledge.

The board decides who the CEO is going to be based on many different factors that not always the employees within the company agree with. The CEO is not necessarily the smartest, savviest, most capable, or most likeable. However, he is the one appointed by the board to give accountability for the company.

Frontline Leadership Meets Husbands' Basic Needs

Husbands have a basic need for admiration and respect, which drives them to be competitive and assume risks, marking their "territory" wherever they go. These qualities may be better suited for frontline leadership, which requires being in the trenches, carrying out the banner, and stepping up in challenging situations. However, it is ironic that when it comes to marriage, some husbands become apathetic and slide their responsibilities under the rug and this becomes a heaping issue for their wives.

Frontline Leadership Exposes our Competence

There are good and bad businesses, but there are also good and bad bosses. Exercising frontline leadership is not about the position, but about the function. When it comes to being a successful leader, the thing that matters is not what we say, but what we do. However, it's not just about taking action. It's about taking the correct action. We need to master the Rules of the Game and model them for the ones we are leading. It is our responsibility to lead them, to set a good example, and to pass on the Rules of the Game with passion and conviction.

In any company, when employees do not know the rules and procedures well and are not clear about their functions stated in the employee handbook, they will be constantly confused. As a result, they will interfere with everyone else's functions.

Similarly, most problems within a family arise from the lack of knowledge of the Rules of the Game. Many people have adopted perspectives and philosophies about marriage that are harmful. This can often result in poorly executed functions and "leadership" that bring pain and resentment to those trying to build a successful and healthy marriage partnership.

Frontline Leadership is about Heading

The function of the head of the house involves leadership. Unfortunately, there is a tendency to misunderstand the concept of "head of the house." Many men create misleading concepts of term "head." Therefore, we prefer to speak of "heading." The first term emphasizes the position "I am the head," and the second emphasizes the role, responsibility, and leadership traits needed. In other words, as husbands, we must lead our family. The idea implies that we must serve in the front line, protecting our families from any threats. This type of leadership is intertwined with men's need for admiration and respect.

The role of CEO is given to the person that is accountable for the success or failure of a business. The CEO is not only the face of the company, but also the one who has to face the consequences when things go wrong. This accountability is required from the frontline leader. Likewise, the husband is accountable for the state of the marriage partnership. He is responsible for its success or failure. Note that I said responsible and not guilty; there is a huge difference between the two.

If your teenage son runs into a neighbor's mailbox with his car, it is most likely that you will have to face your neighbor and make yourself responsible for any damages, even though your son was guilty. The title of husband places the responsibility of frontline leadership in three key areas: physical, psychological, and spiritual. Physically, the husband must lead with every effort to achieve his family's well-being.

He must be able to physically protect his family (with the exception of disabilities), and physically show his affection for them by hugging them, kissing them, etc. Psychologically he should be a motivator, and also provide security and stability. Spiritually, he must be a moral example for his family; his spiritual goal must be to lead with Christ-like behavior if he really wants to see his family blessed. The husband must learn to follow the instructions of his Main Investor. Only through being an example in these three areas—showing, not demanding—can a husband manage to lead the way to a healthy and thriving marriage partnership.

Many husbands think their sole responsibility is to bring home the money, and for the wives to manage it as best as possible. Some people joke about marriages in which wives "wear the pants," but if we're honest, many times men are just absent. Husbands cannot simply shrug off their great responsibilities. Raising and educating children is not the sole responsibility of mothers. Children are the responsibility of both parents. When they excel and succeed, parents proudly declare, "That's my child." But when they call in the middle of the night, one marriage partners will tell the other, "Your child is calling you."

Frontline Leadership is not Imposition

Once, a wise man that was married and had learned the importance of treating his wife well said, "Live with your wives wisely, giving your wives the place they deserve and treating them with care." He knows the importance that wives have in relationships. They are a one-of-a-kind treasure. Husbands must recognize and hold their wives with high esteem and recognize the contributions that they make in their marriage partnership. At the same time they must recognize that in general, women show their emotions more. Women provide a greater contribution in the emotional realm. This characteristic allows them to be the thermostats of their family atmosphere.

Husbands as good frontline leaders must understand that it is essential to encourage their wives to continue developing and performing their leadership roles since building a home demands a mutual and coordinated effort. This can only be achieved by working together as a managerial team.

Men must step up in order to lead the household. Performing their duties makes it certain that wives do not have to take on an additional workload to make up for the husband. Even when wives do it courageously and sacrificially for their need of stability and security, the additional weight on their backs eventually leads them to become stressed. It reaches a point where they blame the husbands for not assuming their share of the burden, or worse, end the marriage because the husband does not assume his responsibilities.

The true role in the managerial team cannot be ignored. Many husbands, for instance, behave as owners rather than CEOs. With this sense of entitlement, they often forget that there is a board that they have to give accountability to. Therefore, the first thing to understand is that CEOs are not the owners. They must do everything bearing in mind that they will be held accountable. They must face the "board of investors," figuratively speaking. When husbands become great and successful frontline leaders, all the parties involved will end up benefiting, and the marriage partnership will also benefit as a whole.

The Pyramid of True Love

Within this model of marriage, husbands ought to love their wives. They must provide everything their wife needs emotionally, spiritually, and physically. Notice we say they "ought to." You may be wondering how someone has the responsibility to love. The thing is that true love is not something you feel but something that you do. Love is not the result of butterflies in your stomach, nor is it the epic romance often times seen in Hollywood flicks. It does not depend on emotion, but on will; it's the product of commitment, not feelings. This love is one characterized by a willingness to give beyond our possibilities. Not measured by current sensations but by continuous actions.

The best way to describe true love is using the model *"Pyramid of True Love of Marriage, Serious Business."* At the bottom we have the *"I'm the owner"* stage. In this stage the individual has his or her well-being as a priority. The implied goal is, "what's in it for me?" In this stage the characteristics of love are: First, physical attraction; second, romance; and third, fixation.

In the middle of the pyramid we have the second stage that we call the *"We are partners"* stage. In this stage the individual has the mutual well-being as priority. The implied goal is, we are partners; therefore, you contribute 50 percent and I contribute the other 50 percent. In this stage the characteristics of love are: first, reciprocity; second, cooperation; and third, consideration.

At the top of the pyramid we have the *"business is first"* stage. In this stage the individual has a greater purpose in mind: the well-being of the business, not the individual desires of the marriage partners. The implied goal and mindset should be to give 100 percent regardless of what my marriage partner contributes, because this business not only has to survive but flourish and profit in all aspects. If the business profits, the partners profit; if the business loses, the partners lose. In this stage the characteristics of love are: first, perseverance; second, wholeheartedness; and third, sacrifice. Our goal as leaders and marriage partners must be to go up the ladder, to escalate to higher characteristics of true love until we get to the utmost and ultimate characteristic in the pyramid, sacrifice.

Conclusion

As previously stated, there are good and bad businesses, and there are good and bad bosses. A good boss is one that listens to his/her employees, looks for their strengths, and helps them develop their full potential.

According to James K. Harter, PhD, Gallup's chief scientist for workplace management, based on a Gallup research that included exit interviews of forty-four organizations and 10,609 business units, at least 75 percent of the reasons why people leave companies have to do with their managers.[26] I wonder how many wives are getting ready to throw in the towel because their husbands are bad CEOs.

Today the great tragedy lies in completely ignoring the role and function that each member must exercise within their marriage partnership. The issue occurs when spouses place emphasis on what the other person should be doing instead of focusing on what they should personally be doing and becoming. Consider what would happen if employees did not have a clear understanding of what their roles and boundaries are. They would constantly interfere with their colleagues' roles and boundaries instead of focusing on their own. Such employees not only fail to contribute to the business, but also make everybody else's lives miserable. Now imagine if it is the boss who ignores his responsibilities and boundaries. It would certainly ensure the failure of the business!

Chris and Carol were going through that same situation. They didn't have a clear understanding of what each of their leadership roles were, and what boundaries they must keep. As a result, they found themselves in a tough spot. They found themselves in competition for control, power, and support from their children. The point is not to try to figure out who was right or wrong, but how they dealt with the situation and how that could have hindered them from figuring out what was best for them.

To succeed in a marriage partnership, we must willingly and consciously decide to become the kind of husbands God wants us to be. By focusing on our roles and responsibilities, we reduce the level of demand and pressure on our marriage partners. This also reduces the degree of frustration with our spouses, and sets the proper perspective— one that facilitates the development of a successful, functional marriage.

Husbands, as CEOs, must lead and take initiative. Husbands, if you have not done so already, now is the time to take lead as the head of the family. To accomplish this, you must first be present. According to the US Census Bureau, [27] black children (55 percent) and Hispanic children (31 percent) were more likely to live with one parent than non-Hispanic white children (21 percent) or Asian children (13 percent). Men must not only show up, but also exercise real frontline leadership at home and develop a family life plan that leads to success.

Now, you must be wondering about wives and their main leadership role in this managerial team. What roles and responsibilities do they have in order to positively influence and change their marriages and families forever?

SOMETHING TO THINK ABOUT
Being the head of the household is not a hat to wear
but an adventure to undertake.

Rule of the Game Seven:
EXERCISE INFLUENTIAL
LEADERSHIP

Objective

That wives, as part of the managerial team, may understand the importance of exercising the unique and specific influential leadership role they have in the *Functional Structure of Marriage, Serious Business*, and how that role could impact and redefine their marriage.

Influence Leadership

A very powerful subtle force that moves not only the hand of man but also his heart.

Marriage Case Study

After several years of marriage, Genie and Charlie have developed a very healthy relationship. Despite Charlie's strong personality, Genie has been very wise in the way she has dealt with her husband throughout their relationship. Whenever they have a strong disagreement, Genie avoids confronting him directly and instead seeks an opportune time to make him see her side of the argument.

"Over the years, I have come to understand that Charlie intuitively responds negatively to any request that I make," says Genie. "Instead of wondering why he acts that way and getting frustrated in the process, I discovered that he later opens up and listens to my reasons or arguments."

"That's what I like about Genie," says Charlie. "She has such a subtle way of introducing a point of view that I had not considered. If there is something I admire about my wife, it's her wisdom. I don't know what would have happened to our marriage if Genie did not share her thoughts so that we can decide together what is best for our family. I have to admit, most of the time she makes a good point."

Obviously, Genie knows how to positively influence her husband when it comes to making important decisions, especially when they could positively or negatively affect the entire family.

"Do not believe it's been easy. Many times, I have asked God to take him before I decide to send him over," Genie says, laughing mischievously. "No, seriously, I do not say that this is the easiest way, but I am convinced it is an effective one. When I see the results, I realize it is worth the teamwork. No wonder some claim that men are the head and women are the neck."

Main Topic

Very few marriages have the intuitive spark to understand what their roles are and figure out a way to make their relationships work in a way that is conducive and beneficial not only for them, but for the entire family, as in the case of Genie and Charlie.

As mentioned in previous Rules of the Game, many couples enter the marriage partnership without really knowing the functions or roles each must play. The Designer of marriage, the one who carefully and skillfully designed us, has established an order in which to run the marriage partnership, which is the basis and foundation of a strong and functional family. That order is what we denominate the *Functional Structure of Marriage, Serious Business.* The one who designed us has given each family member a specific role to play for our own benefit. Family problems arise when the functions assigned to each member of the family are not performed in accordance with the Owner's manual. The Designer's master plan has already been given to us; now we must put it into practice if we want to build a structure that will remain over the course of time.

In order to succeed, we must destroy harmful perceptions, old patterns and habits, and replace them with new ones. It's similar to going to the supermarket and returning with new things; in order to accommodate the new groceries you purchased, you must discard the out-of-date items. In this book, we present a set of rules that constitute the cornerstones of every marriage partnership. The seventh Rule of the Game is to exercise influence leadership in the managerial team.

Influential Leadership Meets Wives' Basic Needs

In the previous rule, we stated that husbands, as CEOs, are responsible for exercising frontline leadership, the kind of leadership that takes the initiative that steps up and is present when most needed, knowing that he is accountable for life's most important investment and endeavor. Husbands assume the frontline leadership not because they are superior, more intelligent, or capable. It is simply the function that fits their basic needs.

The one who designed us knows the psychological makeup of each person, and it is through this knowledge that He has decided to designate the functions of the marriage partnership. If we focus on our roles and understand that every function is essential, we will not find ourselves competing in our marriages because each person will understand, value, and be devoted to fully exercising their own duties.

Influential Leadership Complements the Managerial Team

We know of the fatal consequences of having a living organism with more than one head, or a business with two CEOs with the same authority and functions. Similarly, marriage is a partnership that necessitates only one head. If the husband, as CEO, provides the frontline leadership, what then is the wife's' role in a marriage partnership?

Wives, as COOs managing day-to-day operations, complement their husbands' leadership role by exercising influential leadership, producing an exponential and powerful leadership effect that will benefit the family as a whole. However, we have to be aware that when wives exercise influential leadership, it can bring very positive or negative consequences. Wives have the power to build up or tear down their own marriage partnerships. They have to be aware of the incredible power they have at hand and use it responsibly for the greater good of the business. Therefore, the responsibility of wives is to exercise influential leadership and management in order to maximize and complement their husbands' frontline leadership, for the greater good of the life's most important investment and endeavor. These two types of leadership not only complement each other, but also expand into new frontiers. Wives may communicate more effectively with the leadership of their husbands through subtle influence, rather than openly confronting their husbands. If wives do so, they will achieve the most important and desired goal: the welfare of their marriage partnership.

Influential Leadership Avoids Confrontation

Every home should have a family life plan. This plan should be decided as one, taking into account the Rules of the Game provided by the Designer as well as the needs of each member of the marriage partnership. No plan will succeed if it fails to take these rules into consideration. Wives play a vital role in this decision-making process. Wives who try to face their husbands in a confrontational way are less likely to achieve the desired results. On the other hand, the wives that exercise influential leadership, reacting in a subtle and wise manner, will obtain unimaginable results, however, this way requires much wisdom and self-control though. Most men by nature react competitively to challenges and threats due to their physiological makeup.

Any savvy COO who wants to present an idea to the CEO usually will test the waters first. She will walk by the CEO's office to see if her boss is in a good mood or not. Once the COO perceives it is a good time, she will chat a little bit and subtly present her views. Even more, if the COO is really good, she will make the CEO believe the idea was all his in the first place.

Influential Leadership Improves in Negotiation

Every managerial team should openly discuss the decisions they want to make and list all pros and cons. They must take into account the views of all members, but nothing should be decided based on this list without first comparing it with the Rules of the Game. Just as in many businesses, there are times when you cannot reach a unanimous agreement in the marriage partnership. In these instances the managerial team comes together to try to make important decisions.

Sometimes there are irreconcilable differences. In these cases the CEOs are the ones who have to make the final decision, and they will be responsible before the board for the positive or negative consequences of those decisions.

The other members of the managerial team must put aside their personal interests and opinions for the greater good: the success of the business. There is no business in the world where employees are responsible for the final decision, but they are responsible for expressing their views. They then submit to the decisions made by the CEOs and get behind and rally for the decisions made for the greater good, the wellbeing of the business.

Influential Leadership Enhances Communication

Communication between man and woman has been the subject of discussion and analysis for centuries. The way that men perceive and communicate things is very different from the way women perceive and communicate things. Therefore, both must respond very intelligently to what each is trying to communicate since, in most cases, what is meant is not what is perceived. Understanding these differences is essential for a marriage partnership to run smoothly.

Influential Leadership Feeds Husbands' Basic Needs

Wives feed their husbands' basic needs when they exercise influential leadership since influential leadership is by definition, a respectful way of discussing subjects, sharing ideas, contributing value and ensuring success in life's most important investment and endeavor.

This kind of leadership will maintain access to their husbands and get their ideas and wishes taken into account seriously, as influential leadership complements frontline leadership. Although many times wives may disagree with their husbands, it is essential to preserve the admiration that led them to the altar. It is highly recommended that wives make their husbands feel admired and appreciated for their frontline leadership.

Even though respect may be mutual, influential leadership is the most effective and respectful way of responding to frontline leadership. No matter how logical and practical the COO's opinions are, if they are presented in a defiant and arrogant approach, they will usually be rejected by the CEO, not for the content of the idea but for the way it was presented. Remember, most men react competitively to challenges.

Many wives are getting incredible results. If you are not exercising influential leadership we recommend you give it a try and see the great results, undoubtedly the most effective kind of leadership.

Conclusion

All couples come to the altar with big aspirations, thinking they have found the woman or man of their dreams. The difference between healthy and successful marriages and those that are not is how they accommodate and assimilate the role each plays in the marriage partnership. It is essential to understand that what is at stake is not if we are equal, but simply the success of the marriage partnership. We firmly believe that the Designer of marriage desires that husbands and wives work together, complementing each other and functioning as a managerial team to take their marriage partnership to the next level.

As we saw in the marriage partnership formed by Genie and Charlie, the most successful marriages are those that understand that everyone must conform to their roles if they want to see such an enterprise not only survive, but also flourish. Even when the concept of democracy is very appealing and sounds like the inalienable right of all, it doesn't work like that in the business world. Just imagine the employees voting and deciding by themselves what they want to do or not do in the company just because they are the majority, and in a democracy, the majority wins. Therefore, if husbands are able to understand the serious responsibility they have—not only to themselves but also to their wives, their children, and the Main Investor—then they must lead their families with care, dedication, and seriousness.

Wives who stand next to husbands, who believe in the Rules of the Game provided by the Designer, and live to take the marriage partnership forward, will not have the slightest hesitation following their husbands' frontline leadership. They will respond positively and favorably to their leadership without reservation. Instead of pointing and blaming each other about the bad decisions made in their marriage partnership, husbands and wives must devote themselves seriously and responsibly to actively exercising the appropriate kinds of leadership and focusing on the things that united them. These are the things that should keep marriage partners together, those for which we decided to jump into a lifelong venture and commitment.

However, even when it seems that we have figured it out, that we have deciphered the key to a successful marriage, we shouldn't celebrate victory just yet. Have you ever heard of cognitive dissonance, or how it could seriously hinder and jeopardize your life's most important investment and endeavor?

SOMETHING TO THINK ABOUT
Influential leadership tangoes with frontline leadership.

Rule of the Game Eight:
OWN YOUR INCAPACITIES

Objective
That each marriage partner understands that there is often a contradiction between what we believe and what we do, called cognitive dissonance, and how this contradiction can seriously affect the marriage partnership.

Incapacity
- Lack of physical or mental ability, qualification, or strength to do something or manage your affairs.
- Law; lack of the legal power to act in a specified way; legal disqualification.

Marriage Case Study

Rod and Rachel have very enthusiastically followed the courses of Marriage, Serious Business University and found them revealing, practical, and vital to achieving success in their marriage partnership. However, despite being well aware of the changes needed in their relationship and making serious efforts to implement them, they have failed to fully achieve the desired goals.

"I don't know what's wrong with me," says Rod. "God knows I've made a great effort. I started with enthusiasm and determination. However, soon I was drawn to old habits, which makes me feel guilty and hopeless."

Rod wonders what he can do. He is at a crossroads between what he wants and knows he has to do and what, by instinct or habit, he is dragged back to doing. Rachel, on the other hand, is frustrated, and although progress has been made in many areas, she feels there are certain facets of her life and personality that are unconquerable.

"I never imagined I would experience these emotions and feelings. Sometimes it seems as if I enjoy doing what I am not supposed to do. These feelings of revenge, of getting away with it, of manipulating Rod with my tricks make me feel very bad at the end of the day. Sometimes I wonder how I could do so and worse, how I can continue doing it."

Despite having achieved substantial changes in their way of thinking and perceiving marriage, they feel that something within them keeps preventing them from fully achieving what they want, a sense of failure that destroys any hope of change and success.

Main Topic

Are Rod and Rachel alone? Has anything like this ever happened to us? Come on, let's be honest. My wife and I have been there many times. As a matter of fact, all of us have been in a situation in our lives where we feel we are not going to make it or meet the expectations laid out. Even though we are by nature optimistic as human beings, we are often in the dilemma between wanting something and actually doing it. Today, thousands of dollars are invested in education systems to try to instill the spirit of accomplishment and achievement in children. There are many stories of those that achieve the dreams of fame in sports and entertainment. However, if we do the math, we realize that only one in thousands achieve the dreams they envisioned when they were little. From childhood we are taught to believe that we must achieve success and pursue what we want—the sky is the limit. However, how do you explain why there are more and more children with eating disorders and many more that need psychotropic medication and counseling? Could it be that we are putting on their shoulders a burden impossible to bear? Will the kids soon realize they have real limitations and cannot achieve everything they set out for, as they are led to believe?

The business world is no different. Setting goals and achieving dreams are part of the entrepreneurial spirit, and there is nothing wrong with it. However, every successful entrepreneur knows she cannot do everything. She will focus on her strengths, on those things she know she can do and is good at. Therefore, when starting her business she looks for investors, uses a bank for funds, and recruits human talent to pursue her dreams. Despite the good intentions of every employer to generate wealth and employment opportunities, there is not a single business in the world that can do everything right.

Those who have several years of work experience know that even when many companies know what is best for the environment or their employees, in many instances they do nothing about it. Why? Because this problem of incapacity, manifested in "cognitive dissonance," is part of our nature. We cannot remove it from any human activity. The same applies to any marriage partnership. We often feel overwhelmed by all that we have to do and to deal with, the kids, the meals, the chores, the yard, the leaks, the bills, work, social commitments, you name it. Other times we are unable to do what we must or find ourselves driven to do what harms us. Why does this happen to us? What can we do about it?

In this book we've presented a set of rules that constitute the cornerstones of every marriage partnership. The eighth Rule of the Game is to own your incapacities. Why is it important to recognize our incapacities? Incapacity is a human reality. There are four basic sources of incapacity.

Incapacity by Nature

The first is by nature; that is, the physical constitution with which we were designed. We all remember the famous story of the tortoise that wanted to fly. This tortoise used to dream day and night of achieving that goal. However, there was a vital problem inherent to her desire. By nature she had not been endowed with wings to fly. In other words, she was unable to reach her dreams because her physical composition did not allow her to. This is incapacity by nature.

Incapacity by Lack of Skills

The second is by lack of skills; that is, the motor and mental skills to properly perform a specific function. In this area, people have made great efforts and reached great achievements. The Special Olympics and other similar events, for example, show that people with disabilities can achieve great goals. However, in spite of the progress in this field, not everybody was born with all the skills; and even when many skills can be developed, there are limitations to those skills. For instance, not everybody has the skills to be an athlete; not everyone can compete professionally in the NBA or MLB or the FIFA World Cup. This is incapacity by lack of skill.

Incapacity by Lack of Knowledge

The third is by lack of knowledge; that is, the necessary information to properly perform a function. There was a TV show in the late 1990s called The Pretender, which featured a genius who could assume any identity and profession he wanted, possessed a photographic memory, and could read hundreds of pages in seconds. This character had everything by nature—skill and knowledge. Obviously, he's a TV personality, and although there are many "pretenders" in the world, the reality is that sooner or later they will find themselves at a dead end. It is essential to understand that there are areas of specialization we will never be able to carry out because of our limitations and incapacities. Although the human brain is equipped to amass tons of information and knowledge, it still has limitations. This is incapacity by lack of knowledge.

I remember back in the 1990s when I visited some friends in Chicago. They were really busy and told me to feel free to take the bus, go downtown to see the city, and visit some museums and landmarks. They gave me a map (no GPS in those days), and there I was, petrified that I might make a wrong turn and end up in one of those neighborhoods where you don't know if you will make it out alive. All these fears were rooted in my lack of knowledge of this particular city. This incapacity hindered me from navigating and enjoying such a beautiful city as I do my hometown.

Incapacity by Legal Ruling

The fourth is by legal ruling, that is, the inability to do something due to a legal ruling. For example, in many countries, citizens cannot do most legal work on their own; for that, they need to hire a lawyer, who, by law, has the legal capacity to act or proceed with such formalities. This is incapacity by legal ruling. The incapacity of which we speak here is not so much to the lack of skills or knowledge, but of restrictions provided by the law. People with this kind of incapacity don't have anything wrong in terms of skills or capacity, but a legal issue hinders them from enjoying the benefits or services provided by the law.

Someone once told me about this person in Latin America who was related to a member of the drug cartels. He was a decent, law-abiding citizen who lived a normal life. One day he decided to take a trip to Spain with his wife and children. He went through the tedious process of getting their passports, obtaining a visa to Spain, and buying the tickets. After weeks of planning and working hard, they were finally at the doors of the airport, full of excitement for the long-awaited adventure. After he presented his passport to the customs officer, he continued to check in regularly until he noticed the officer looking back and forth from his passport and him. The officer made a couple of calls and a few special agents showed up. They led him to a private room where they started to interrogate him. After several hours they let him know that he had a legal impediment that prevented him from leaving the country.

"A legal impediment?" he asked with disbelief.

"Yes sir," a special agent noted. "All the members of your family have legal impediments preventing them from leaving the country."

The man raised his voice, frustrated and disappointed, "But I already have my passport, visa, and tickets. What do you want me to do?"

The special agent told him, "Sir, there is nothing we can do. You have to solve this legal issue in a court."

We all have a legal issue to solve, a legal impediment with our Creator that we need to fix first if we want to go out there and enjoy all the benefits of a free person.

Cognitive Dissonance

Cognitive dissonance is a state of unrest and frustration produced by the contradiction that exists between what you know is good and what you do in opposition to that which is good; that is, the contradiction between our beliefs and our behavior. For example, if I know it's bad to eat saturated fat foods but my body drags me out to the fast food restaurant to eat the largest order of French fries, I'm going against what I know is best for me. As a result I will feel guilty for being unable to control my own impulses. Let's ask ourselves, how can I know what is good but often not be capable of doing it? If you have ever been in a situation like this, you are facing the condition called cognitive dissonance.

Many years ago Saul of Tarsus, also known as Paul, wrote, "The honest truth is I do not understand why I behave as I do, so instead of doing the good I want, I end up doing the bad I do not want. Now, although I do what I do not want to do, I recognize that the instructions that God left for us are for our good. I can well admit that, although there is a part of me that wants to do what is good, my nature, which has been damaged and marked by an uncontrollable desire to do evil, drags me to do the contrary. I know that this nature inside me, damaged and marked by selfishness, will not let me do the good I want because, although I have every intention of doing so, I simply am incapable. I do the wrong I do not want to do rather than the good that I want to do. I've concluded that, even if I have all the desire and willingness to do good by nature, in the end, I can only do what harms me." [28]

Whether we accept it or not, we all come marked with a nature that disables us from doing what really benefits us. It's like when a car manufacturer launches a new line of vehicles and soon after he realizes that they come with a factory defect. Immediately the manufacturer calls for all people who have that type of vehicle to return it to the dealers as soon as possible to repair the defect before a tragedy occurs.

Similarly, we could say that we come with a manufacturing defect, a defect that was introduced when our first parents made bad decisions. This manufacturing defect is a strong inclination that draws us to do what is not for our best, what we know will harm us. It is an inclination that prevents us from doing all the time what we know is right and beneficial for us. Since then, all human beings struggle day to day with this manufacturing defect. We believe it is important for us to be aware of this reality as by doing so we will head in the right direction. This will allow us to find a solution to our incapacities and may pave a new understanding of our human reality and the need of a true internal power source that generates the strength and energy for a real change.

Conclusion

What Rod and Rachel underwent is shared by many individuals and couples at some point in their lives. The twists of life, those things that are beyond our control, such as illness and accidents, make us realize that we are unable to control all facets of our lives. It is important to recognize that we are unable to control not only our external circumstances but also our inner drives that lead us to do what we do not want. The Designer of marriage, the Main Investor, wants us to realize our incapacities not to make us feel bad but so we return to the manufacturer who has what it takes to fix this manufacturing defect. This manufacturing defect, which consists of an inner nature, damaged and scarred by an uncontrollable desire to do evil and manifests in an incapacity to do the right thing, can only be repaired by the manufacturer. He can give us a new nature with the ability to do what really is helpful and beneficial, not only for us as individuals but also for our marriage partnerships.

Such a change is the product of an understanding of our human reality and the result of a personal experience with God. That search leads us to an understanding of the legal and spiritual state in which we find ourselves before our Creator and what He did for us to solve that problem.

In addition, once we understand that the Designer of marriage has placed us in this time and place in history to carry out a unique mission, we will be able to experience what it means to live a life of true fulfillment and meaning. We recommend our book, The Flip Side of Jesus, which analyzes Jesus from a different angle, as human, as leader, as someone that displays the greatest human example of mission and purpose and how we can discover the very reason we are on this earth answering to basic human uncertainties: Where do I come from? Where am I going? And what am I doing here? It raises the legal issue we have with God and how we can solve it.

The important thing about the cognitive dissonance is not to point out what we are not capable of but how we can manage our weaknesses. Do you want to know how the concept of threefold cord can radically change how we manage our weaknesses and how it can change our marriage partnership forever?

SOMETHING TO THINK ABOUT
Incapacity is the divine instrument the Manufacturer
uses to make us look up to heaven.

Rule of the Game Nine:
BECOME A THREEFOLD CORD

Objective

That each marriage partner will understand that the most solid and stable position for the marriage partnership is at the junction of three, known as the "threefold cord."

Threefold cord

A braided rope made of three ropes carefully intertwined and linked together to form a very resistant and powerful unit.

Marriage Case Study

Art and Stephanie approached their twenty-fifth anniversary. Looking back, they were able to remember great moments. Some were marked by joy and happiness, as the wedding of their eldest daughter and the birth of their first grandson. Others were marked with pain and bitterness, as in all the fighting and hurtful words that were said. Both are convinced that the fundamental reason they still stand together, fighting for their home and children, stems from a decision made soon after marriage, a decision that forever changed the way they viewed their lives and marriage.

"When Art and I fought and insulted each other, we distanced ourselves for days. It was as if the whole world collapsed in an instant before me. The disappointment and bitterness were gnawing away my heart. This further distanced us, and secretly we were blaming each other. Our home was abruptly headed toward failure, throwing out the window all the good times and dreams we had," Stephanie whispered with tears in her eyes.

Both Art and Stephanie had lost not only the north in their marriages but also their desire to fight for it, until their friends shared a secret, one that made it easier and gave them a sense of purpose and meaning.

"After we learned the concept of the threefold cord, our marriage took a turn in meaning and significance; we found the inner strength to fight for our home and to do whatever necessary to stay together," said Art with a radiant smile of hope and certainty.

Art and Stephanie's marriage exemplifies that one new revelation, perspective, or insight might help you get ahead.

Main Topic

The number three has been the subject of intrigue and mystery. We do not know what it is, but from a simple triangle to sophisticated pyramids, we've found a concept of stability, completeness, and performance in the number three. That same concept is found in the figure of the Trinity, one God in three persons with different functions but the same essence. Whether it's the incomprehensible mystery of the Trinity, the appealing wonders of a pyramid, or the basic elements of engineering, three is an essential prime number. Think what life would be like if there were only two-legged chairs or if earth were missing one of the three essential elements—fire, water, and air—or if a three-piston engine would run only on two pistons.

As we continue to talk about the Rules of the Game that constitute the cornerstones of every marriage partnership. The ninth Rule of the Game is to become a threefold cord. The threefold cord rule establishes a truth without which the marriage partnership cannot flourish; that the contract made at the altar the day we married was made—consciously or not—not only between husband and wife but also between God, husband, and wife. That is, our marriage is a powerful partnership between three parties; it is a sturdy braid with three ropes, and this is what we mean by threefold cord. Just as Art and Stephanie, the sooner we realize and embody this concept in our marriages, the sooner we will experience a prosperous and successful married life with happy members; with physically, emotionally, and spiritually healthy children; and with a new worldview.

Sense of Stability

The concept of threefold cord brings a sense of stability. When we mentioned the contrast between a two-legged chair and a three-legged one, we wanted to emphasize this idea. Simply adding a third leg to the chair provides a sense of stability that is essential for the chair's function; that is, the chair was made to be sat on. Very few people would be willing to sit on a chair with two legs. However, people will sit confidently in a chair with three legs because they know a three-legged chair guarantees the stability needed to stay safe and secure. In the same way, the marriage partnership, when firmly established on three strong legs, produces a sense of security and stability that will confidently support others in it. Above all, we must have this kind of marriage partnership so our children have a safe place to lean on and a model to follow and replicate.

Sense of Totality

The concept of threefold cord provides a sense of totality. When we mentioned what would happen in the absence of one of earth's three essential elements—fire, water, and air—we wanted to emphasize this idea of totality. Just imagine what would happen on planet Earth without one of these three essential elements. In the same way, the marriage partnership will develop a sense of totality that brings satisfaction and purpose to family life when all three parties actively participate.

Sense of Performance

The concept of threefold cord produces a sense of performance. When we mentioned the three-piston engine that runs with only two pistons, we wanted to emphasize this idea of performance; that is, an engine that was designed to operate with three pistons but runs with only two does not perform to its full potential. In the same way, the marriage partnership will never be able reach its full potential while running on only two pistons. You must activate the "third piston." As we can see, the threefold cord rule provides a sense of stability, totality, and performance. These are the key ingredients of every human activity and enterprise, particularly the most important business of all: the marriage partnership. Those who have experienced the effectiveness of this Rule of the Game feel the need to share it with their friends and relatives because it transforms marriage from a constant nightmare to the most exciting and extraordinary entrepreneurial adventure of our time on this earth.

Conclusion

Art and Stephanie, in spite of all the fighting and hurtful words, the distance and bitterness, the gnawing and blaming, were able to find a path that changed their marriage partnership forever. Just like Art stated, "After we learned the concept of the threefold cord, our marriage took a turn in meaning and significance; we found the inner strength to fight for our home and to do whatever is necessary to stay together." Now don't get me wrong. I am not saying that including God in the equation— who by far is the most interested party in our success—guarantees absence of conflict, dissolution, frustration, and disappointment, among many other things. However, it brings a sense of stability, totality, and performance that provide the purpose and energy necessary to keep trying, to keep moving, and to make it work.

The principle of threefold cord is one of the cornerstones of the marriage partnership. Although this concept has not been widely disseminated, it is precisely what has made a difference in hundreds and thousands of homes that have intuitively understood and applied it. We all know deep in our hearts that in addition to the physical world we see, there is also a spiritual world. If we want a strong and successful marriage partnership we must maintain a balance between the material and spiritual worlds. Failure to do so would be like taking the bike, valued at one million dollars, built by manufacturer Koga Miyata for the Dutch cyclist Theo Bos (who competed during the Olympics in Beijing), and not putting on one of the tires. How far would Bos be able to go with only one tire? Would he be able to win a medal? Would he even be able to cross the line?

A life in which we serve only material desires and neglect spiritual needs is like having the world's most expensive bike—but with only one tire. We will not get very far! Understanding that the marriage partnership is a partnership between three parties, God, husband, and wife, helps us forge a new vision and perception of God as the main shareholder and investor, and the one who is most interested that we carry on a legacy to our children and grandchildren for generations to come. Do you want to know what kind of legacy to leave behind?

SOMETHING TO THINK ABOUT
*When it comes to our marriage partnership, the most
ignored shareholder happens to be the most interested one.*

Rule of the Game Ten:
LEAVE A LEGACY BEHIND

Objective
That each partner understands that the marriage partnership must prevail in order to leave a solid legacy to its successors and the world.

Legacy
- From Latin legatia, legatus, meaning "ambassador, envoy."
- That which is left to or handed down from a predecessor to successors, whether a material or immaterial thing.

Marriage Case Study

The bustle, the infant cries, the contagious laughter, and the unstoppable dances flood the entire house. Max and Margot are the unifying force in the Altamirano family. Undoubtedly, Max and Margot are the pride of the whole family. No wonder they have left a strong impact on the lives and hearts of all their children, grandchildren, and great grandchildren.

"My parents have been an example of hard work and dedication," said Berenice, the Altamirano's eldest daughter. "I will be grateful my entire life for the example they have left us."

"If there is something I have to thank my parents for, it is the heritage of a stable, rooted home throughout all these years," says Carl, the youngest child. "Can there be a better legacy for the whole family than this?"

Both Max and Margot decided very early in their marriage that they would provide better opportunities for their children than they had. They decided to build a strong marriage to be a sanctuary from the wild world in which they lived, to become a meeting place for family warmth.

Main Topic

Even before all the big corporations existed, even before the industrial revolution and the establishment of the Ottoman, Roman, and Greek empires, even before the formation of the nations, there was the marriage partnership. Many companies come and go; they appear at dawn's heat and fade at cold dusk. But those that stand the test of time and the shaking of the economy are the ones engraved on the pages of history as the great testaments to perseverance and dedication. Such is the case of one of the oldest family businesses in the world, Hoshi Ryokan, founded in Japan in AD 718. Or Chateau de Goulaine, a business dedicated to producing wine, founded in France in AD 1000.

Every family business produces goods, whether tangible or intangible that contributes directly to the common good. This production is generated by a sense of survival that generates an inner strength and the release of human talent and ingenuity, and by a sense of transcendence with which we have been marked—something that leads us not only to bring the "bread" to the table but also evokes a strong desire to leave something behind for the future generations.

The Main Investor, who believed in our potential and gave us freedom of choice, instilled this deep sense of transcendence within us, a sense that produces a continuous and urgent need to undertake something that will remain. In this book we present a series of rules that constitute the cornerstones of the marriage partnership. The tenth Rule of the Game is to leave a legacy behind. Men and women come together in a marriage partnership to undertake something that endures, that transcends. But what is this idea of undertaking something that endures, that transcends, all about? What are the true implications of this rule? What do we want to undertake? What does it mean to leave behind something that remains?

In this search for purpose and meaning, we all go through this world with a desire to make an impact and find purpose and meaning. The universal human search for purpose and meaning indicates that the reason we are placed on this earth is to leave a footprint, a legacy for our loved ones. The size of the footprint we leave behind depends on how aware we are of the ephemeral nature of our stay here, the value we place on human life, the sense of the eternal, and that spark of curiosity and ingenuity that God has placed in us all. Regardless of the size of that footprint, all of us, sooner or later, want to give continuity to our lives, our thoughts, and our achievements. We want to capture this continuity in our children first and foremost, whether we decide to have them or if we have the joy of receiving them. We want to see accomplished in them the fullness of our achievements.

However, we are often wrong in what we can and must pass on as a legacy. Many today believe that the best legacy we can pass on to our children is education or a career. Now don't get me wrong; I am not against education or a career. As a matter of fact, I promote them. Although having an education or a career is a great goal in life, it is not the most important legacy we can leave to our children. For example, we have all heard from parents who want to impose on their children their own career paths, their own dreams, or their desire that someone carry on the family business. They do this without taking into account their children's personal life goals and preferences, not knowing if they have been placed on this planet with a mission very different from that of their parents. We firmly believe that the legacy of which we speak is not one imposed by force, one that neutralizes the dreams and preferences of our children, but precisely that which helps build and develop their own skills and aspirations.

A Legacy of a Successful Marriage Partnership Model

The first and most important legacy we can leave to our children—and the world—is a successful marriage partnership model. Today, successful and happy marriages, those that stay together, are considered an endangered species and a rare thing. Just think of married couples you know who have been together for years and who are successful and happy. Think of all that they have contributed to making people around them happy: their children, grandchildren, and other relatives. Think of the admiration and respect they receive from their own family and others. These intangible benefits, such as happiness, love, stability, self-esteem, and a sense of identity and belonging, are priceless. The impacts that a single marriage partnership can have on an entire community or even an entire society are incalculable. How much more so a network of successful marriage partnerships determined to rescue the distorted image of marriage and willing to carry this message of restoration and hope to a hurting society immersed in confusion and despair.

A Legacy of Good Men and Women

The second kind of legacy is essential for the formation of good men and women. If there is anything that this world desperately needs, it is just that. But how can we define what makes a good man or woman? Although it is a very broad concept, we can say that good men and women are people who deeply value individuals for their intrinsic worth—people who have a high regard for the full development of a society that promotes free exercise of fundamental rights, solidarity, generosity, honesty, and hard work. Good men and women are designed with an internal impulse that moves them to act for and on behalf of the common good. Good men and women are not just good people with good intentions, but good people with concrete actions that distinguish them as such.

How can we raise children to become good men and women? There is not a formula to ensure that result. In fact, one of the great mysteries of life is to see children of extraordinary parents going astray and becoming selfish men and women and also to see children of terribly bad parents becoming good men and women. However, we can safely say that, generally speaking, we are going to reap what we sow. If you follow the Rules of the Game, planting in the hearts of your children a life of dedication, hard work, good intentions, and appreciation for people, they will germinate the seed that produces good men and women. We must not forget that this seed produces a tree that can take years to yield its first crops. You may have to prune it many times before seeing it yield the desired quality and abundance. Home is the factory of good men and women. To produce good men and women, we must teach and model to them the *5 Great Codes of Life*: obedience, faith, wisdom, honor, and generosity that we will discuss in later publications.

A Legacy of a Unique Identity Brand

The third kind of legacy is a unique identity brand that represents our marriage partnerships, something that defines us as family and that we can leave to our children, our communities, or the world. This unique identity brand will provide an antidote for our children during the difficult teenage years. This unique identity brand provides a sense of belonging and pride that will protect them from peer pressures and detrimental trends.

There are families throughout history who have been known for some contribution to their communities or, in other cases, for leaving a legacy of evil behind them. Although not all families achieve the fame or infamy of the Kennedys, Medicis, or the Borgias, we all leave a legacy to our children, our families, and our communities. Some of these legacies will stand the test of time and pass from generation to generation. Others have only a temporary impact and will be forgotten.

Medical science is paying attention to the health history of our ancestors more than ever. Studies indicate that if our ancestors had certain conditions, we most likely have a good chance of having them too. What a nice legacy they have left us, don't you think? But the scary thing is that we also pass them onto our children. The same is said of mental illness and even what some call "generational sins," which are transmitted from generation to generation, as in the case of teen pregnancy, alcoholism, or physical abuse, among many other legacies. There are things we cannot evade; they're in our DNA and are part of our family line. However, the legacy to which we refer here is based on the things we can change. If we are to leave a legacy for our future generations, including a successful marriage partnership model, the formation of good men and women, and a unique identity brand that defines us as a family, we will help forge a better future not only for them but also for the entire world.

Conclusion

All of the great institutions—from large and well-known ones, such as Oxford University or the Red Cross or Manchester United, to even the small and unknown ones—are legacies that past generations have left us. Perhaps we are not aware of it, but we all breathe, move, and live in the midst of legacies. While it is true that we all leave a trace behind, the kind of footprint we want to leave is a positive impact on the lives of our children through the life of our marriage partnership. The kind of footprint that Margot and Max Altamirano have left in the lives of their children and grandchildren, one that is priceless. Just think about how the screaming and playing of their grandchildren, warm chats of their children, and their own magnetic personalities make everyone feel happy and fortunate. The admiration, respect, and affection of young and old for Margot and Max during family reunions make it much more than a home; they form a footprint, a legacy for future generations.

Like the Altamiranos, we should all set our hearts on leaving a legacy that will prevail over all the superficial distractions that capture our daily attention and entrapped us—a legacy that is beyond properties, businesses, jewelry, or academic degrees. A legacy that is sealed in the minds and hearts of our successors as if engraved on a platinum plate. One that no one can remove from our souls and allow our children to see the marriage partnership as serious business, as the most important investment and endeavor in life, one that produces good men and women who live by the *5 Great Codes of Life* and makes them proud of carrying a name, like an insignia, worthy of respect and admiration. That is the greatest challenge of our generation!

SOMETHING TO THINK ABOUT

*The legacy we pass on to our children is
a step that could put them above or below us.*

ABOUT THE AUTHORS

Lawrence and Xinia Otarola have been married for almost thirty years and have three wonderful children. They are speakers, writers, and producers of the radio and television program *Marriage, Serious Business* for Spanish speakers and now for the English-speaking world as well.

Lawrence earned his bachelor's degree in business administration from the Universidad Interamericana de Costa Rica and a master's in leadership and organizational change at Pfeiffer University. Lawrence has a very interesting combination of business, education, and ministry experience that has propelled a movement in favor of family.

Xinia is a mother and an educator by vocation, earning her bachelor's degree from Universidad Estatal a Distancia in Costa Rica, and currently teaches at Charlotte Latin School in Charlotte, North Carolina. She is a very talented TV host and has a God-given gift to encourage and motivate others.

For more information or to schedule conferences and presentations, visit their website at www.marriageseriousbusiness.com and find out why, when it comes to marriage, they mean very serious business!

NOTES

1   The Small Business Administration Office of Advocacy, www.sba.
gov/advo

2   Brian Tracy, "Getting Rich Your Own Way: Achieve All Your
Financial Goals Faster Than You Ever Thought Possible," *Wiley; 1st
edition* (February 17, 2006)

3   Linda J. Waite and Maggie Gallagher, "Why Married People Are
Happier, Healthier, and Better Off Financially" *Broadway Books,
New York, NY.* (2000)

4   Robert H. Coombs, "Marital Status and Personal Well-Being: A
Literature Review," *British Journal of Medical Psychology* 40 (1991):
97.

5   "Disaster Planning." *Https://www.sba.gov/content/disaster-planning.*
Www.sba.gov, n.d. Web. 20 Jan. 2016.

6   David Popenoe, PhD, "The Future of Marriage in America,"
*University of Virginia/National Marriage Project/The State of Our
Unions*, (2007)

7   Larry L. Bumpass, James A. Sweet, and Andrew Cherlin, "The Role of Cohabitation in Declining Rates of Marriage," *Journal of Marriage and the Family,* Vol. 53, (1991): 913-927

8   David Popenoe, PhD, The National Marriage Project, University of Virginia (December 2011)

9   Bramlett and W.D. Mosher, "Cohabitation, Marriage, Divorce and Remarriage in the United States, MD"

10 National Center for Health Statistics, Hyattsville, MD (September 1985)

11 Ibid.

12 Peter F. Drucker, "Management Challenge for the 21st Century," *HarperBusiness 1st edition* (June 2001)

13 Justin Rosenstein, https://blog.asana.com/2011/10/every-step/

14 Coombs, "Marital Status and Personal Well-Being," 97.

15 Balakrishnan, T. R., K. Vaninadha Rao, Evelyne Lapierre-Adamcyk, and Karol J. Krotki, "A Hazard Model of the Co-variaters of Marriage Dissolution in Canada," *Demography* 24 (1987): 395-406.

16 Andrew M. Greeley, *Faithful Attraction: Discovering Intimacy, Love and Fidelity in American Marriage* (New York: Tom Doherty Associates, 1991).

17 Yllo, Kersti, and Murray A. Straus, "Interpersonal Violence Among Married and Cohabiting Couples," *Family Relations* 30 (1981): 343.

18 Ibid.

19 Steven L. McShane and Mary Ann Von Glinow, "Organizational Behavior, Emerging Realities for the Workplace Revolution" *McGraw-Hill Irwin* 4th edition (2008): 5.

20 Ibid.

21   Steven L. McShane and Mary Ann Von Glinow, "Organizational Behavior, Emerging Realities for the Workplace Revolution" *McGraw-Hill Irwin* 4th edition (2008): 14.

22   Steven L. McShane and Mary Ann Von Glinow, "Organizational Behavior, Emerging Realities for the Workplace Revolution" *McGraw-Hill Irwin* 4th edition (2008): 14.

23   Steven L. McShane and Mary Ann Von Glinow, "Organizational Behavior, Emerging Realities for the Workplace Revolution" *McGraw-Hill Irwin* 4th edition (2008): 14.

24   Jesus of Nazareth, (Luke 12:34)

25   N. Nicholson, "Evolutionary Psychology: Toward a New View of Human Nature and Organizational Society," *Human Relations* 50 (September 1997): 1053-78; B. D. Pierce and R. White, "The Evolution of Social Structure: Why Biology Matters," *Academy of Management Review* 24 (October 1999): 843-53; Lawrence and Nohria, *Driven: How Human Nature Shapes Our Choices.*

26   Robison, Jennifer. "Turning Around Employee Turnover." Gallup. com. Business Journal, 8 May 2008. Web. 30 Aug. 2015.

27   Jonathan Vespa, Jamie M. Lewis, and Rose M. Kreide, "America's Families and Living Arrangements: 2012," (August 2013): P20-570

28   Saul of Tarsus (Romans 7:15-21 Paraphrased)